TRADING PLACES

RADIUS

TRADING PLACES

John Palmer

RADIUS

An imprint of Century Hutchinson

An imprint of Century Hutchinson Ltd
62–65 Chandos Place, London WC2N 4NW

Century Hutchinson Australia Pty Ltd
P O Box 496, 16–22 Church Street, Hawthorn,
Victoria 3122, Australia

Century Hutchinson New Zealand Ltd
P O Box 40–086, Glenfield, Auckland 10
New Zealand

Century Hutchinson South Africa (Pty) Ltd
P O Box 337, Bergvlei 2012, South Africa

First published by Radius 1988
Published in association with Granada Television

© John Palmer

Printed and bound in Great Britain by
Mackays of Chatham Ltd

British Library Cataloguing in Publication Data

Palmer, John, *1938–*
    Trading places: the future of the European Community:
    a companion to the Granada
    Television series.
    1. European Community countries. Economic
    conditions. Influence of economic policies
    of European Community.
    I. Title
    330.94

    ISBN 0–09–173187–9 Pbk
    ISBN 0–09–173182–8

Contents

Trading Places is a companion volume to the Granada Television series of the same name.

The publishers gratefully acknowledge the assistance of:
Presenter   Paul Heiney
Producer   Michael Ryan
Director   Peter Swain
Researchers   Colin Bell
                                     Jan Elson
                                     Alison Rooper
Executive Producer   Rod Caird

Preface

An old friend of mine, prominent in challenging established thinking about the technological revolution of the past twenty years often says: 'The future is not like a coastline over the horizon waiting there to be discovered. The future has to be *made*, by the choices of men and women in society.' His point is that there is not one, but many different potential futures.

It is an insight which inspires this book. Having been professionally involved in European affairs for the greater part of the last twelve years — as the European Editor of *The Guardian* newspaper — I greatly welcomed Granada Television's initiative in making a series of programmes examining some of the stereotypes trotted out in almost any popular discussion about the European Community. I was also very pleased to be asked by Granada and by Radius, the new imprint of Century Hutchinson, to write an accompanying book which would take up some of the themes of the television series *Trading Places*. In it I have tried to sketch out the decisions which may confront Europeans in the relatively few years that remain of the twentieth century.

I am reminded of that old and ambiguous Chinese saying, 'May you live in exciting times' when reviewing the current European scene. Although media attention focuses on the (seemingly) unchanging problems of the European Community, the 1990s promise to be years of profound change in Europe. The changing relations between the super-powers; the prospects for significant arms reductions in Europe; the movement for reform in the Soviet Union; the restless desire of many Europeans — east and west — to recast the map of a divided continent drawn at Yalta forty years ago; the challenge to European society of the world economic crisis: all give the idea of Europe a new significance and relevance.

It has been possible to set out only some of the pressing issues which the European Community must confront in the coming decade. The television series and this book will have served their purpose if they help to ensure that the debate in Britain about the future of Europe and the European Community is better informed than it might otherwise have been.

I am grateful to Andrew Robinson, Michael Ryan and their colleagues at Granada for helping to bring this project about and for their generous assistance during the writing of the book. I would also like to thank my editor, Neil Belton at Radius, for maintaining a clarity of view and perspective when deadlines threatened to overwhelm. A special word of thanks is deserved by my colleague in Brussels, Andrew Garfield, EEC correspondent of *The Scotsman*, for his invaluable help and by Bill Martin and Peter Wragg of the European Commission. Last, but certainly not least, I am grateful to my long-suffering family for tolerating those weekends spent in the company of a word processer.

John Palmer
January 1988

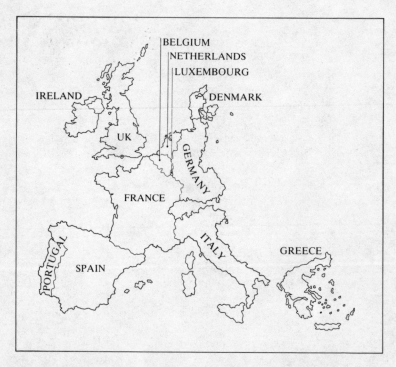

The Community of twelve after Greece, Portugal and Spain became members (1981–1986).

Source: European Commission

1
European Problems

How recognizable will the economic, political and social face of the European continent be at the start of the Third Millennium? Change and a sense of new choices are in the air for the peoples of Europe.

This book is about the different futures unfolding in Europe and the challenges they will present to orthodox values and views. A brief look at the world in 1988 reveals the scale of the coming changes which Europe cannot escape.

Perhaps the most dramatic sign of change has been the agreement between the leaders of the United States and the Soviet Union of the first ever treaty that would actually reduce the vast arsenals of nuclear weapons held by the super powers. For a few optimists the agreement presages the end of a Cold War which has divided Europe for forty years and made it the most likely arena for nuclear war.

Others take a less euphoric view. What if the abolition of medium range nuclear missiles is followed by the progressive abolition of all other nuclear weapons based on the continent? How will Europe defend itself in a future which may see the gradual withdrawal of the American military presence?[1] Is there still a 'threat' from the Soviet Union and its allies, or should Europeans be seeking a comprehensive political settlement which would disarm and gradually unite Europe from the Atlantic to the Urals?

There is no doubting the pressure for change in both halves of divided Europe. The European Community now embraces twelve of the nations of Western Europe — Belgium, Britain, Denmark, France, Greece, Holland, Ireland, Italy, Luxembourg, Portugal,

Spain and West Germany — and is planning to eliminate the remaining barriers to a fully free trade market by 1992. The west European countries which are members of the European Free Trade Association — Austria, Finland, Iceland, Norway, Sweden and Switzerland — seek ever closer relations with the EEC, in a 'European Economic Space' which would cover eighteen countries and more than 350 million people.

The impulse towards unity is in part a reflection of the huge scale of the economic problems now facing modern industrial societies. As the stock market crash of October 1987 so dramatically underlined, the developed world, and certainly the whole of western Europe, already shares common economic dilemmas and is criss-crossed by identical trans-national financial and industrial networks.

But as the world faces the prospect of renewed economic recession in the early 1990s, new answers will have to be found to the old problems of unemployment, inflation, industrial decline and the decay of social provision as well as Europe's inability to counter the growing commercial challenge from the United States, Japan and the 'economic tigers' of the Pacific Rim.

The years to the end of the century will offer Europeans the choice of strengthening a mainly free market based economic system or of developing new forms of accountable economic planning and democratic decision making. Politicians and economic writers are now united in agreeing that the old form of mixed economy, with its emphasis on bureaucracy, centralization and national planning from above, cannot be restored. Indeed, the incapacity of the state, under almost any political dispensation, to provide answers to the global economic crisis is already leading to suggestions that decision-making be transferred from the national state: upwards to the European Community, and downwards to the local communities and regions whose historical and political legitimacy is only now being rediscovered.

The forces of change at work in Eastern Europe are even more dramatic. The emergence of Mikhail Gorbachev in the Soviet Union, and the policies of *glasnost* (openness) and *perestroika* (restructuring) — combined with a readiness to consider the scrapping of the military apparatus of the Cold War — promises more thorough-going reform in the eastern-bloc countries than has been seen for fifty years.

Yet the winds of political change mingle uneasily with the storms of economic crisis. Deepseated economic problems are highlighted by a growing appetite for political democracy. The combination of political reform and productive stagnation in Eastern Europe is taking forms that could not have been predicted. Closer links are already being established between the EEC and COMECON, the eastern bloc trading organization, which may prefigure a more fundamental move to pan-European integration.[2]

But if there is to be greater European unity, how will this express itself? What kind of society could Europeans dream of building in common? What kind of role should the new Europe play in the wider world? Could Europe break with its two super power patrons and create a new force for non-alignment and political change in the world at large?

Meanwhile, how are such aspirations to be measured against the palpable incapacity of the European institutions to solve their existing problems? The European Community is gripped by the most serious financial crisis in its thirty-year history and is seemingly incapable of agreement on the most basic and obvious reforms of its spending policies, or on how to provide itself with the resources and authority needed to tackle precisely those economic and social problems which have defeated so many of the individual member states.

The chapters that follow are not intended to spell out blueprints for this or that type of change. Rather they seek to understand the nature of the challenges which now face the peoples of a continent still deeply divided by history, national culture, language, ideology and social systems. They will ask — is the very concept of European unity a chimera, or a necessity for the world of the 21st century?

The political rediscovery of Europe is, then, a strange but exciting story. The European Community stands at the very heart of this renewal. There can be no discussion about the future of the wider geo-political thing called 'Europe' without coming to terms with

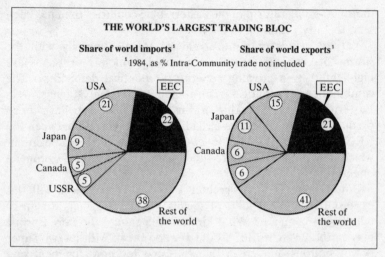

THE WORLD'S LARGEST TRADING BLOC

Share of world imports[1]   Share of world exports[1]

[1] 1984, as % Intra-Community trade not included

The Community's share of world imports and exports exceeds that of the USA or Japan.

Source: Eurostat

the key role of the European Community. Its creation and development have shaped so much of western European life during the past thirty years.

The 'Common Market', as it is more commonly known in Britain, has, in the years since 1957, grown from a limited association of six founding member-states to a complex economic and political institution which includes twelve countries. And the Community now exercises a major influence over the economic, industrial and even the foreign policies of those remaining western European states in the European Free Trade Association which still remain outside its formal membership.

The EEC, with its more than 300 million people, is the capitalist world's largest trading bloc, and without doubt a major international economic power. There has been a dramatic shift in the balance of economic power between the United States and the European Community during the past twenty years. European dependence and subordination in the post-Second World War

14

period has given way to European insistence on co-equal status with the US on the world stage.

There are other ways of measuring this hesitant assertion of autonomy in economic and political affairs. As we shall see the creation of the European Monetary System, which seeks to link together the exchange rates of the key EEC currencies and promises to be a step on the road to full European Monetary Union, was inspired by the disillusion of EEC governments with the irresponsible manner in which successive American administrations managed the affairs of the US economy and, specifically, the US dollar.

The European Monetary System has provided some limited degree of insulation from the backwash created by the persistent turbulence around the dollar. But the EMS is only as strong as the participating governments' resolve to support each other's currencies in moments of difficulty.

The past decade has provided ample evidence of the extent to which European industry is falling behind that of Japan, the other Asian industrialized countries and, to a degree, that of the United States. A modest start has been made in reducing Europe's technological backwardness and thus in closing the competitive gap with Japanese and American big business. We shall examine the effectiveness of the Community's attempt to catch up, and ask whether European culture and society might not inspire a distinctive approach to technology and its uses.

The 1980s have been years of international commercial conflict and the EEC came close to open trade war with both Japan and the United States. In the case of the US, the issues in dispute have ranged from the struggle to dominate international grain markets, to European subsidies for the Airbus and the growing temptation of trade protectionism in the United States.

We shall look at these conflicts and ask whether they do not indicate that the international economic order laid down under US leadership after 1945 is slowly disintegrating and ask what this means for Europe. Have European governments yet grappled with the implications of the challenge to the international monetary system and to the General Agreement on Tariffs and Trade (GATT, the watch-dog body on international free trade) stemming from the decline of US financial ascendancy and from the slide to trade protectionism?

While its economic maturity is undeniable the political character of the European Community is far less well developed. But there have been major developments in what is largely termed 'political cooperation' among EEC countries in the past ten years which have brought closer the goal of a common foreign policy. The twelve EEC member states now invariably take common positions in the United Nations and, on occasions, launch common foreign policy initiatives — as on the Israeli–Arab conflict in 1979 or on southern Africa, where they have agreed to seek political change in the apartheid regime.

In the aftermath of the INF (Intermediate Nuclear Force) agreement between the United States and the Soviet Union, the debate about a more self-sufficient policy for European defence has grown more clamorous. Some EEC and European NATO governments, alarmed at the possible decline of the American military presence in western Europe have revived the Western European Union, as a forum for thrashing out a common European defence policy and building a 'stronger European pillar' within the NATO alliance.

We shall look at the radically different options open to Europe in the post-INF age and ask whether western Europe should try to perpetuate the Cold War alliances and seek to compensate for a possible US withdrawal from Europe by building a more independent military nuclear force.

This sense of change, of challenge, of movement is far from being the image of the European Community in the minds of most European, and certainly most British people. The popular perception of the EEC is of near bankruptcy, discredited policies, a remote and impenetrable bureaucracy, of political infighting between the national states and ineffectiveness in world affairs. If there is one image of the Common Market which, more than any other, symbolises its failure it is the monstrous food mountains which have been accumulated and maintained at such cost while millions starve in the African Sahel.

In later chapters we will analyse the root cause of the agricultural crisis and the related threat to the entire budget of the

16

European Community. But as well as examining what changes need to be made in existing EEC policies such as the Common Agricultural Policy, we will ask what additional policies Community member states should be developing to face more effectively the challenges of economic crisis, industrial decline and social need.

The goal of an internal market permitting free trade, free movement of capital and of persons by 1992 is obviously an important one. But we shall ask whether there is not also a need for a 'citizens' Europe' or a 'social Europe' where consumers' and workers' rights, civil liberties and social standards are increasingly standardized at the highest levels obtaining throughout the Community. Certainly the absence of a significant human dimension in the European Community has weakened the sense of identity between it and the peoples of its member states.

The British were, with the Danes, the least enthusiastic entrants into the European Community.[3] The decision to join was only taken after referenda which exposed large minorities who were, and have remained hostile to the supra-national pretensions of the EEC and who look back nostalgically to the days of national seclusion.

British politicians from Enoch Powell, on the right, to Labour's Michael Foot and the Communist Party on the left, reacted to the prospect of EEC membership with dismay. Powell spoke of the creeping 'subjugation' of the British people by the Brussels Eurocracy. There was, he ventured in 1971, 'one simple question: to be or not to be, to be ourselves or not to be ourselves'. Foot and others bemoaned the threat to 'national sovereignty and Parliamentary democracy' in having decisions taken by the EEC Council of Ministers and by the European Court of Justice, beyond the control of Britain's juridical and Parliamentary institutions.

But to what extent have economic and political developments turned national sovereignty into a shadow of its former self? Under Mrs Thatcher even the pro-EEC Conservative government has espoused a form of national Gaullism in relations with the EEC, for instance over negotiations about the terms of Britain's net contribution to the Community budget.

The stridency and — in the eyes of some other Europeans —

excessively narrow and nationalist bias of this approach to EEC affairs was summed up after an EEC summit in Dublin in 1981 when Mrs Thatcher thumped the table at a press conference to underline her determination to secure control of 'our' money. She was referring to the UK contribution to what, in Community theory at any rate, is intended to be a common pool to finance the development of the Community.

Of course the British have not been the only people to play the national card at the European table. All EEC member states, when it suits them, are ready to use their national veto over developments favoured by the others, even if this obstructs important common European policy projects. The French have done so over farm expenditure, as have Italy and Greece, while West Germany has used its power to block increased spending on non-farm expenditure.

The fact remains that the English retain a sourer and more suspicious attitude to things European than most other peoples. It is difficult not to see in this the lingering effects of an island, and imperial, history. Perhaps this also explains the relatively lukewarm response in Britain to the construction of a Channel Tunnel link with 'the continent', a project that has aroused enthusiasm in France. Certainly it seems to explain British reluctance to participate fully in a range of joint ventures, such as the European Space Agency.

Less is heard today of demands for British withdrawal from the Community. But there are still widespread objections to any new transfer of powers from the national to the European level, as envisaged under recent amendments to the Treaty of Rome. Equally striking is the way in which the aspirations of the directly elected European Parliament to have a bigger say in decision-making have been resisted not only by the government but by Westminster parliamentarians.

In the minds of many people, the European Community is personified by a vast, insensitive international bureaucracy, determined to impose a uniform way of living on the citizens of Europe without regard to local needs and traditions. This leviathan is supposedly inspired by a dogma of European integration whose bible is EEC's founding Treaty of Rome. To the man or woman in the street, the European Commission in Brussels is obsessed with a harmonization programme that threatens 'the British pint', the national taste in sausages and the British style in lawnmowers.

The level of public knowledge and understanding of this monster, and how it works, leaves much to be desired. To some extent the European institutions have themselves to blame for the boredom their very mention can induce. They have not alone failed to convey basic factual information about themselves but also any clear sense of the Community's aspirations for the future of European society.

The episodic hostility of the British to the EEC is not usually duplicated in other EEC countries, apart from Denmark. This may have something to do with a lingering popular identification of the EEC with the cause of peace in Europe. The British, whose territory has been spared the horror of a modern land war, often find it difficult to appreciate the determination of Germans or Italians to avoid internal conflict within Europe.

But enthusiasm for Europe is on the decline even in the heartland of the Community, the Benelux countries (Belgium, Holland and Luxembourg), Italy and West Germany. Strikingly, however, the same polls reveal a remarkable degree of public support for the idea of greater European unity including, in one poll published by the Commission in 1987, a European government.

But the low level of discussion about the Community also reflects on the state of the British media. While the 'quality' press does pay a degree of attention to European affairs, its foreign-news priorities still reflect the post-war attachment to the United States.

The mass circulation newspapers pay virtually no attention to European affairs except where stories of 'waste', or some threat to a hallowed British tradition, or the lifestyle of members of the European Parliament, can be turned into sensational copy. More pernicious has been the incitement of national prejudices by newspapers such as *The Sun*, which sponsor campaigns against the perfidy of the 'Frogs' or other Continental riff-raff. In this way archaic national stereotypes — owing more to the 1790s than the 1990s — are reinforced.

The record of television in covering European affairs has also been less than impressive. Coverage of what might strictly be defined as European Community news, and political, economic and social affairs in other European countries is intermittent and inconsistent. It is hardly anti-American to point out that the British can more easily imagine life in Dallas or New York than in Dortmund or Naples, given their diet of popular media culture.

Membership of the European Community is now an organic part of what Harold Wilson called 'the governance of Britain'. The range of national policy decisions where the European Community's agreement is legally necessary (or at any rate which must not be incompatible with existing Community law) is very great. The integration of Britain into the Community has reached the point where unilateral disengagement would raise enormous administrative and legal problems, as well as economic and political problems.[4]

The impact of the European Community on our national life will, moreover, increase significantly in the years ahead. In part this will be a result of the Single European Act, an amendment to the Treaty of Rome agreed by all twelve member states during 1986 and 1987.[5]

Under the SEA there will be less opportunity for individual countries to plead an 'overriding national interest' as justification for wielding a veto to block majority decisions in the Council of Ministers. Taken together with a strengthening of the consultative rights and powers of amendment of the European Parliament, and a redefinition of the European Commission's day-to-day authority to manage Common Market affairs, the Single European Act represents a further, albeit very modest shift of political power from the nation state to the Community.

The justification for the SEA lies in part in a desire to resume progress towards the original goal of the EEC and the treaty of Rome, namely a progressive strengthening of the unity and effectiveness of the Community and its institutions. But it also reflects frustration with the ineffectiveness of those institutions, dominated as they have been by the overweening power of the nation state.

An even more dramatic development has been the decision by the twelve national governments to complete the common market, which the EEC first set out to achieve thirty years ago. But while the customs barriers have come down, many other obstacles to a fully integrated market remain and have even increased in recent years due to national decisions on taxation, technical standards and other matters.

Commitment to the full internal market will mean that all remaining fetters on the freedom of trade should disappear by 1992. The consequences are only beginning to be understood. For example, public sector purchasing policy will have to operate on strictly free market principles and state subsidies to industry will disappear. This will, at a stroke, remove some of the most important instruments that governments in the past have used to regulate national economic and industrial policy.

One important effect of these developments is that the old debate about the Common Market — whether or not Britain should have joined it and whether it should now remain a member — is dying on its feet. Even those who are most dismissive of the Community's works and pomps no longer really believe there can be a future for an isolated Britain outside the EEC.

The loss of empire; the decline of the Commonwealth; the erosion of Britain's 'special relationship' with the United States; the obvious attraction of the EEC even for those EFTA countries which were once thought to provide a potential alternative grouping for Britain in Europe: all these changes have contributed to the erosion of support for withdrawal as a serious strategy.[6] We have moved a long way from the world of 1947, when the Labour Foreign Secretary could tell the House of Commons, 'His Majesty's Government does not accept the view . . . that we have ceased to be a great power, or that we have ceased to play that role.'

In 1950 a Labour National Executive Committee statement recorded the party's belief in the 'spiritual unity' of the former Empire territories now in the Commonwealth and observed ' . . . we are much closer in all respects except distance, to Australia and New Zealand, than we are to Western Europe.' In the same year the Labour cabinet minister Hugh Dalton said of Western Europe: 'You need us; we do not need you.'[7] It was an attitude

21

that prevailed within the Labour Party even after the attempts by successive governments (those of Macmillan, Heath and Wilson) to obtain terms for joining the European Community, and still influences the approach of the Labour Left.

Although British Conservatives and representatives of British industry were quicker than Labour to abandon the illusion that the Commonwealth could, in the long run, provide better markets for British industry than those becoming available in Western Europe, Anthony Eden could still appeal to President Eisenhower in the early 1950s not to push Britain towards the emerging European Community since this ran 'counter to its instincts.'[9]

Even in 1962, Mr Peter Walker — now a member of Mrs Thatcher's government — wrote that Commonwealth trade ties would prevent Britain being caught up in the EEC and added that the mere possibility of Common Market membership would be 'a great gain for Communism.'[10] Ironically since then the majority of right and centre right opinion has agreed that there is no alternative for Britain but to be part of, and to seek to exert its influence within, a larger geographical and political power structure.

At the other end of the political spectrum, 'Europe' — far from being a problem for radicals — has in recent years become a rallying point for the peace movement, militant ecologists, feminists and the post-1968 left. Trade unionists have also become involved in Europe-wide organizations to defend jobs and conditions and to press for reduced working hours.

The European Community has always been a conundrum for Labour. On the one hand there is recognition that withdrawal is no longer an easy or convincing option, as Mr Neil Kinnock recognised after the election defeat of October 1979.

On the other hand the European Community could — given the commitment to complete the internal market — evolve in directions which would bring it into open conflict with a future Labour government. As we have seen, the dismantling of national economic controls whether over foreign trade, investment or the movement of capital, will in all probability be a *fait accompli* by the time of the next British general election.[8]

No matter which ideological vantage-point it is viewed from, the economic prospects for Europe in the 1990s look far from rosy. There is no indication that the cycle of ever-longer recessions and ever-shallower periods of economic expansion, which have marked the world economic system since the early 1970s, has come to a halt. The international pressure on many of Europe's traditional manufacturing industries, on which Britain and other countries have so heavily depended for the employment of their peoples, seems likely to continue and even to intensify.

There is a continuing shift in manufacturing industry from Western Europe — and northern areas of the United States — to the countries of the Pacific Rim and, to a degree, to Latin America. If world growth falters — tripped up by the Third World's mounting debt crisis and the US budget deficit, the struggle for markets is bound to get worse in the next decade.

Whatever collective power the European Community can bring to bear to counter this trend and to develop alternative industries (and thus sources of new jobs) individual national economies will be more, not less, vulnerable to the forces of global economic change. We need to think about the kind of policies Europe should adopt to face these global challenges, as well as what changes in its political institutions the European Community will have to make to be able to implement its strategies.

The irony is that the European Community will play a vastly more important role in our lives at a time when many of its policies, notably the Common Agricultural Policy, are in crisis, when it faces something close to financial bankruptcy, and when there is a question mark over its capacity to respond to a rapidly changing world situation.

The contrast between the failures and incoherence of the present European Community and the urgent need for effective, supra-national bodies that can inspire a common European response, is a reflection of imperfections in real life. If the European Community did not now exist it, or something very like it, would have to be invented by the individual EEC member states.

The magnitude of the EEC's failures will be all too apparent in later chapters. The first and most obvious of them is the constant threat of collapse in the Community budget. The unstoppable growth of expenditure on the Common Agricultural Policy means

23

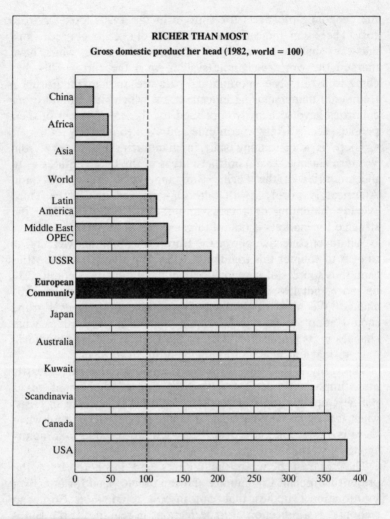

RICHER THAN MOST

Gross domestic product her head (1982, world = 100)

The graph shows that the European Community's wealth — measured in terms of GDP per head of population — is about 270 per cent of the world average. The graph conceals wide disparities in Community living standards: the average Greek, Irish or southern Italian citizen disposes of less than half the wealth of a Luxemburger or resident of Munich, and is much less likely to own a car or telephone.

Source: Eurostat

that farm spending now accounts for £18 billion, more than 70 per cent of the annual budget.

In the closing months of 1987 it appeared that the final budget crisis had been reached as the EEC awoke to the prospect of having insufficient revenue to meet even the Community's legal obligations, and thus no means of funding a deficit of around £5 billion.[11] Despite efforts to curb agricultural overproduction, the slump in the value of the dollar had the effect (as we will see later) of pushing up the cost of subsidising surplus food exports to markets in which the price of food is much cheaper than in the European Community.

The legal ceiling on the Community's budget revenues (drawn mainly from transfers by the member states of Customs duties and agricultural levies as well as a notional proportion of the average of VAT turnover throughout the twelve), has been obviously insufficient for a long time. The cause lies not only in the open ended nature of the commitment to maintain agricultural prices — only now being modified to take account of overproduction and the notorious food 'mountains' — but also in pressure to meet the needs of disadvantaged regions and social groups, as well as the demand for increased EEC research and development.

When the CAP was set up, the Community's founders were anxious to increase agricultural productivity in order to meet postwar Europe's fear of food shortages and to guarantee farming communities a reasonable income. The idea was to produce food in sufficient quantities to give the Community a prudential reserve, as an insurance policy against harvest failure or emergency shortages. In the early days much stress was put on the wider social value of sustaining small or family farms.

The reality has been different. The primary beneficiaries of the CAP system under which producers have been guaranteed high and fixed prices for their output have not been the small peasant farmers — beloved of the CAP's evangelists — but the very largest farmers, including the new breed of agricultural corporation.

The EEC farm regime unwittingly speeded up the human onslaught on the environment through excessive use of the pesticides and fertilisers that set off the output explosion of the past twenty years. The resulting excess of food over the market demand for it and the allied policy of subsidised dumping of food outside Europe have helped to undermine farmers in Third World countries, undercutting their prices on world markets. The policy has, in this way, stoked demands for agricultural protectionism and increased trade tensions, as we shall see, in the cases of grain, oils and fats.

If the non-farming sectors of the European economy were in a healthier state and if the prospects for overall economic growth were brighter, one could expect to absorb the farming population displaced from agriculture without too much difficulty. But this is far from being the case.

Indeed, the second major crisis facing the EEC is the collapse of its traditional employment-giving industries. In later chapters we will look at some specific cases: notably steel, textiles and shipbuilding. What they all have in common is a history of sharp decline, so that productive capacity is a fraction of what it was only a few years ago.

The Treaty of Rome has commonly been read as a free market document, yet the EEC has in practice attempted to regulate the decline and restructuring of these industries through arrangements that seek to restrict the free play of the market. This has been most striking in the case of the Community's steel policy which includes both external protection from cheap steel imports and a market sharing cartel fixing production quotas and minimum prices.

If the recessions which have hit the market for steel during the past fifteen years showed signs of passing, the interventionist regime of the EEC might have been able to prove itself, despite the massive loss of jobs. But with the 1990s almost upon us, the EEC is now having to make further cutbacks in steel-making capacity which will strain Community solidarity to its limits.

As if these tribulations were not enough, the European econ-omies are all saddled with the human and financial costs of high and persistent levels of unemployment. There are more than seventeen million out of work in the EEC and some twenty million in Western Europe as a whole. The social security costs involved — even though governments have reduced the value of dole payments — are the biggest single element in pushing national budgets into deficit. But the deficits have made EEC governments even less ready to spend on common policies, as disputes over the level of research, regional and social expenditure reveal.

There are also big divergences in the ability of the different EEC economies to respond to the challenges of external competition, the full internal free market and industrial restructuring. So serious is the potential drawing-apart of the EEC economies, that unless counterbalanced by conscious efforts to increase cohesion, the freedom to buy and sell wherever one likes on the internal market could simply enhance the advantages of the richer regions. The Greek, Irish, Portuguese and Spanish governments have already warned that they will not tolerate a liberalisation of trade that drains the Community's peripheral regions of capital and labour resources for the benefit of the highly developed heartlands of the EEC.

That is why the Commission wishes to strengthen the European Monetary System, which binds the exchange rates of most of the EEC currencies together. This will in turn require a far greater willingness by national governments to coordinate their economic and financial policies. Otherwise the EMS will not survive. This danger is also present as a result of the disruptive impact of the dollar's decline in value on the different European currencies. But economic and monetary 'convergence' — let alone the goal of economic and monetary 'union' — may prove utopian, given the extreme reluctance of national governments to cede monetary authority to the EEC.

It is far from clear whether the twelve will even be willing to strengthen the supranational, central-banking aspect of the EMS. Opposition has been fiercest from the West German authorities, who fear that sharing power over monetary and credit policy with other governments might weaken the Federal Republic's fanatical commitment to a policy which puts the containment of inflation above all else. Other EEC governments, they fear, might put growth or employment before such stern priorities.

However Britain (with the other poorest EEC countries, Greece, Portugal and Spain) has yet even to allow sterling to be fixed to the EMS currencies. The differences in competitiveness between the weaker, mainly southern countries and the richer northern countries are considerable. When the EEC finally liberates capital movements from all remaining controls, will the EMS be able to withstand the strains?

The economic gap between the richer and poorer regions of the Community presents a fourth set of awesome problems. Some of the southern European states have, as we have seen, indicated that their support for liberalisation of trade and capital movements may depend on a parallel agreement to double the level of expenditure on the Community's 'structural funds' — that is, its spending on regional and social development.

The European Commission President, Mr Jacques Delors, a former finance minister in the French Socialist government, has already said that without a marked strengthening of the EMS — in effect the creation of an EEC central bank — and a boost for spending to assist the most disadvantaged regions, the completion of the internal market could be in jeopardy.

There is no shortage of other problems. The EEC may be able to respond effectively to the challenge from its technologically advanced competitors such as Japan, but the jury is still out. In the brief period in which the Community has been financing major research and development programmes — which will be examined later — some successes have been claimed, for example in the field of telecommunications technology.

Criticism of the management of the EEC research effort as a whole, and in particular the ESA (European Space Agency) programme, has been cited by the British government to justify its insistence on a sharply reduced level of spending on research. This led, between 1986 and 1987, to a cut of almost fifty per cent in the original Commission proposal for a budget of £7300 million. But in spite of the successes of research projects such as ESPRIT (information technologies) and BRITE (application of new technology to traditional manufacturing industries) the total EEC effort is still dwarfed by those of Japan and the United States. Advances in US technology benefit from the Strategic Defence Initiative programme — 'Star Wars'. Although Japan has proposed a vast research project comparable in cost to SDI, devoted to civil and social needs — such as disease eradication and the prevention of desertification — nothing on that scale has even been considered by the EEC.

The argument over the EEC's spending policies has been embittered and immensely complicated by a separate though related dispute over the planned reform of the EEC budget. There is general agreement that the system must be overhauled and that a curb must be put on the rate of spending growth, so that it does not rise faster than revenues; and also that, specifically, the share of the budget accounted for by farm spending — now more than seventy per cent — must be reduced. There are of course differences as to how this should be achieved. Once again it is Britain, along with West Germany, which is least enthusiastic about raising the revenue ceiling of the EEC budget. It is no coincidence that these two countries make by far the biggest net contribution to the Community finances. Britain's position, however, has been alleviated by agreements, negotiated in the late 1970s and early 1980s, which return to the UK the greater part of its annual payments to Brussels. Yet the pattern of EEC spending, with its very heavy bias in favour of agriculture, does not offer Britain much in the way of benefits to counter-balance expenditure outside Britain.

The problem is made worse by the Conservative government's distaste for public spending programmes, whether at national or European level. There is also little doubt that the intractability of the budget conflict between London and Brussels — and the bruising summit encounters between Mrs Thatcher and her EEC colleagues, which she appears to relish — have done more than any other issue to sour popular taste for the EEC in Britain.

Let us glance, finally, at some external problems facing the Community. They go to the heart of the Community's economic relations with the other major non-Communist industrial powers — the United States and Japan. Relations between the Europeans and their principal trading partners have never been so bad, in the whole period since the Second World War, as they are now. Trade and currency frictions are seriously weakening the commitment of the US and the EEC to the trading and monetary institutions developed after the war to monitor and supervise the international economic order.

The General Agreement on Tariffs and Trade (GATT) and the Organisation for Economic Cooperation and Development (OECD) have both warned of trends which could make the 1990s a decade of protectionism and international trade conflict. The EEC is already under intense criticism for its protectionist policies, and not only in agriculture. In their turn EEC governments have warned that if the United States Congress adopts what it sees as the dangerously protectionist Trade Bill during 1988, outright trade conflict may become unavoidable.

Addressing the European Parliament in November 1987, the Commission President, Jacques Delors, warned that the most worrying signs of global economic collapse were the astronomic American budget and foreign trade deficits, the Third World debt burden and the chronic trade surpluses of Japan and some of the other newly industrialized economies of the Pacific.[12] Mr. Delors's magisterial survey could also have noted that during the 1970s and 1980s the EEC itself has adopted external trade policies sharply at variance with its commitment to internal free trade. Import controls have been applied to steel and other products, while public-sector contract guidelines have been adopted, in the telecommunications sector among others, which effectively discriminate against non-European companies.[13] More aggressive use has been made of anti-dumping measures to curb Japanese imports into the EEC, while quotas and tariffs are still imposed on a range of non-EEC imports such as textiles, in an attempt to limit the damage done by cheap imports from the Far East and eastern Europe. The pressure for trade protection reflects the role of imports as a repayment for unemployment.

In spite of the fact that the EEC swears by the global trade–liberalisation objectives set for the current 'Uruguay Round' of GATT negotiations, it might not take too radical a drop in the world economic temperature to send the Community running towards a 'Fortress Europe' strategy. If unemployment increases again during the 1990s, reversing the slight reductions in some EEC countries in the late 1980s, demand for Community-wide import controls could become intense.

For how long will the European Community authorities be able to sustain a contradictory commitment to internal liberalisation and external protectionism? The answer will depend on whether the GATT negotiations end in disagreement, with a stalling of the thrust towards world trade liberalisation. But it will also depend, most crucially, on whether the major western governments can agree on a strategy for the world economy that avoids a further serious recession.

During the past ten years a major integration of European business has begun. As we shall see later, European companies are already anticipating the completion of the internal market and the past few years have seen a dramatic upsurge in cross-border take-overs and mergers between European corporations. Interestingly it has been Italian companies, such as Olivetti and IRI and — at the other end of Europe — Scandinavian corporations like Swedish Match and Ericsson that have set the pace for European acquisitions and takeovers in the consumer-durable and electronics sectors. But large European companies are by no means certain whether their merger strategy should be a global one — aimed at American and Japanese companies offering strengths not available in Europe — or a narrower strategy designed to produce independent trans-national companies of sufficient size, technological clout and diversity to withstand the competitive challenge of the Americans and Japanese.[14]

Many large European companies now have major investments in the United States and therefore have a strong interest in avoiding general trade conflict between the western industrial superpowers. European business organisations such as The Round Table — dealt with later — will press strongly for a European Community committed not just to internal but to global free trade.

By contrast, industrialists in sectors such as steel, textiles (and to a degree cars and shipbuilding) insist that some discrimination in favour of weak or developing European industries is justified. Others argue that to develop hi-tech skills comparable to the US and Japan, European industry must be given protection and state support to allow it to evolve to the point where it can face unrestricted competition.

*

On the face of it, the debate about the European Community's future, whether internally or in its relations with the rest of the world, appears to be an affair of economists and statisticians. But within the economic indicators lie vital political options, choices to be made about the kind of society Europeans wish to live in. The trouble is that the Community appears to have little to do with 'politics' in the conventional sense of the word. For example the EEC plays only the most marginal role in key areas of interest to ordinary people — social services, education, health, pensions, taxation or the great issues of peace and freedom. Responsibility for decisions in these fields are jealously guarded by national states.

It is remarkable that the political agenda for the European Community is still set largely by big business and its political sympathisers. This is reflected in the way in which priorities for the full internal market have been drawn up. There has been very little debate about any alternative agenda, one concerned with imbalances of opportunity in the national communities of Europe.

A fresh agenda would raise questions very relevant to the Europeans' daily lives. Why, for example, should the Community insist that the same laws on competition or the free movement of capital should apply in Birmingham as in Bremen, in Cork as in Copenhagen, yet tolerate stark differences in living standards, basic social services and retirement pensions, and wildly different regulations for health and safety at work?

The irony is that the trade unions, the Labour Party and other groups with a vested interest in such questions have been so preoccupied with the old issue of Britain's membership of the Common Market, that they have given hardly a thought to the real political challenge of Europe. The centre and the right have been free to set the terms in which the region is discussed. We will examine later whether the controversies around the internal market may not stimulate a greater variety of political agendas for Europe in the 1990s.

Meanwhile the European Community is increasingly involved with the high politics of foreign, security and defence policy. Reference has already been made to the development of 'political cooperation' between the twelve. On the one hand exciting changes in the world situation — for instance the new relationship between the nuclear super-powers — push the European governments towards a single European foreign and security policy. On the other hand, nothing divides European public opinion so deeply as foreign and defence policy. At present there is a quiet consensus among EEC *governments*. But if elections return to office governments committed to comprehensive nuclear disarmament and non-alignment, the facade of European political unity will be difficult to maintain.

Ignoring the reservations of some member states (notably Ireland, with its tradition of neutrality between the Cold War alliances) the EEC is actively trying to develop a common policy on disarmament and security. The more narrowly military aspects of this are dealt with by the Western European Union, a group of seven European NATO states revived in recent years as a forum for hammering out a European defence strategy.

Significantly the WEU forum excludes both the United States as well as the European neutrals, and even European NATO governments such as Denmark and Greece, whose commitment to NATO orthodoxy on the first use of nuclear weapons is thought to be less than wholehearted.[15] Here the key discussions are taking place about 'strengthening the European pillar of NATO'. Here too the proper European response to the super-power agreement of December 1987 is argued out and Gorbachev's detente strategy is analysed. But the WEU is above all concerned with the possible rundown of the American defence guarantee for Western Europe.

One immediate issue for the WEU forum is whether Western Europe — in the shape of the big EEC countries — should develop some joint nuclear weapons capacity. A clearly related question is what scale of conventional and nuclear defence will be appropriate for Europe in the 1990s. The right and centre right governments in power in the majority of European NATO states are determined to preserve the unity of NATO and the continued 'coupling' of American and European security.

There are serious differences even within this uniformly conservative group of governments. These concern the priority to be given to the nuclear as opposed to the conventional element in NATO's European arsenal, the feasibility of a purely European nuclear force (some governments are sceptical), and the tactics that should be pursued in future arms negotiations with the Soviet Union.

This could prove to be an issue that divides West Germany from its British and French allies. The Christian Democrat/Liberal coalition in Bonn (and of course the Social Democratic and Green opposition parties to a much greater extent) want to follow any withdrawal of Soviet and US medium-range missiles with an agreement to eliminate short-range and battlefield nuclear weapons which, by definition, are likely to fall only on German soil in the event of war. The British and French, however, fear that the removal of these weapons after the INF missiles have gone may push western Europe further down the dangerous road of 'denuclearisation'.

Even when WEU and NATO governments are agreed about the importance of maintaining strong conventional forces, some are extremely reluctant to find the resources to meet even minimum NATO targets for military spending. NATO leaders repeatedly warned during the 1980s about the shortfall on what they believe are the spending levels needed to maintain NATO's fighting effectiveness.

Not only Denmark, which has long fallen down on its NATO budget commitments, but even 'loyalist' states such as West Germany are having difficulty finding the resources needed to maintain the current pace of arms spending; and Belgium, meanwhile, in 1987, pleaded financial difficulties for its decision not to replace its nuclear air defence system with the American NIKE missile.

The pressure to find more resources would become far greater in the event of a sudden American rundown of its commitments to the defence of western Europe. The current governmental consensus is in favour of a high and rising level of arms spending well into the 1990s. That was the reasserted position of the seven WEU states — Belgium, Britain, France, Holland, Italy, Luxembourg and West Germany — at the meeting of their foreign and defence ministers in The Hague in October 1987.

The European peace movement, and a large section of the left and centre left parties in western Europe, take a very different

view of the future. They see the limited super-power agreement
on medium-range nuclear weapons, combined with the arrival of
Gorbachev and the mounting pressures on all countries' defence
budgets, as providing a rare opportunity to negotiate away all
nuclear weapons systems from European soil.

Opinion polls, including one sponsored in 1987 by the United
States government information service, indicate that a growing
number of Europeans believe that the United States rather than
the Soviet Union has been responsible for the past lack of progress
in arms reduction negotiations.[16] And there is some support in
Europe — notably on the radical and 'Green' left — for the
complete dismantling of both NATO and the Warsaw Pact.

The strictly military inter-governmental debates on European
security take place, as we have seen, in the non-EEC Western
European Union. But the European Community itself is increasingly involved in security discussions, as well as the more narrowly
economic and industrial aspects of how to integrate western
Europe's defence industries; this is justified by the Community's
responsibility for industrial policy. Some WEU governments,
notably that of Belgium, would like to abolish the distinction
between the WEU and EEC aspects of European security
policy — a development that would not only be embarrassing for
Ireland, in view of its non-aligned position, but also for NATO
dissidents like Denmark and Greece.

If a US withdrawal from Europe forms one nightmare for European leaders, an only slightly less gruesome prospect for them
would be an American decision to persist with the Star Wars
project. Many European governments are convinced it cannot
work, and they fear it will both de-stabilise relations between the
super-powers and further undermine NATO's doctrine of flexible
response in a 'limited' European war.

The European political agenda will therefore be highly charged
in the years ahead. This throws into even sharper relief the underdeveloped state of the political debate in Britain about European
politics. It might help to start with a description of the political
geography of the European Community and its institutions: how
it works, who takes the decisions, where the power lies in Brussels,
Luxembourg and Strasbourg and in what ways the Community's

decision-making institutions are changing. We may then be able to cast more light in later chapters on the state of agriculture, industry, politics and trade — and on the future evolution of Europe as a whole.

2
Inside the Eurocracy

One of the more uncomfortable and over-priced flights in Europe is, without doubt, the Brussels–London route.[1] It is uncomfortable because the planes that fly back and forth every few hours are invariably full to capacity. They are mainly filled by men and women flying to meetings of the European institutions that take decisions which shape our daily lives.

Yet remarkably little is known, by the people who pay for them, about the power these EEC institutions now wield. The European Commission, the Council of Ministers, the European Court and the European Parliament are only some of the more visible bodies that exercise the 'governance' of the European Community.

There are, in addition, a hundred and one lesser-known committees. Some are subsidiaries or offshoots of the Commission, or the Council, others are committees of governmental 'experts' and some are 'consultative' bodies such as the Economic and Social Committee of the EEC, which groups together industrialists, trade union leaders, farmers' organizations and a range of professional bodies. Some are more powerful than others, but their numbers have grown dramatically, not only with the expansion of the Community from its original six, to nine, then to ten and now to twelve members but also as a result of the huge expansion in the range of issues that now concern the Community.

In any one week, on their way from Heathrow or Gatwick to Brussels Zaventem airport, can be found senior civil servants meeting to agree on a new draft directive on Value Added Tax, scientists from the member states concerned with agreeing a common research and development programme, central bank

Trading Places

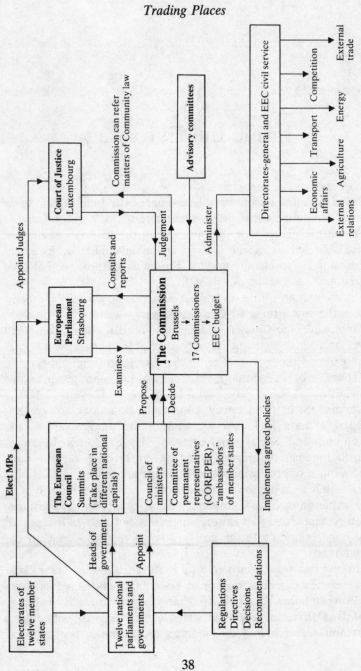

The European Bureaucracy.

officials heading for a regular meeting to review the operation of the European Monetary System, and health experts concerned to agree common regulations on the labelling of food.

These and a hundred and one other detailed policy matters are the day-to-day stuff of European Community government. The meetings to which the overwhelming majority of the officials, experts and specialists attend will go unnoticed by the general public. The media will not report their proceedings and will rarely appreciate the significance of their conclusions.

All this activity seems sometimes to confirm the perception of the European Community as one vast bureaucratic leviathan with tentacles stretching into our very homes. This is, however, some-what misleading. The overwhelming majority of the bureaucrats who are concerned with Community affairs on a regular basis are part of their national governmental machines, not of the EEC as such.

The Commission: a leviathan?

The European Commission itself is quite a small body — as can be confirmed by a visit to the Berlaymont, its Brussels head-quarters. It employs fewer executives than one of Britain's larger local authorities. At present it employs some 12,000 people, but some 1,300 of these are simply concerned with language — with interpretation and translation. This is not really surprising considering that the twelve member states use a total of nine 'official' languages, a definition that denies formal status to a range of minority languages spoken within the EEC.

In some ways the Commission is a far less powerful body than its public reputation in Britain suggests. Its power is limited to proposing policies for adoption by the decision-making Council of Ministers. It is, together with the European Court of Justice, the guardian of the Treaty of Rome, the EEC's constitution and was established at the foundation of the European Community in 1957 as the supra-national executive responsible for the day-to-day management of the Community. Thirty years ago, it is true, the Commission enjoyed far greater political prestige than it does today and was expected by many people gradually to evolve into an embryo government of a united Europe.

The 'Founding Fathers' of the Community, as they came to be known, were an unusually far-sighted and strategically-minded group of centre-right politicians who exercised great influence in their own countries in the post-war period. They included the veteran French finance minister, Jean Monnet, his cabinet colleague, foreign minister Robert Schuman, the Italian prime minister, Alcide de Gaspari, the first Chancellor of the Federal German Republic, Konrad Adanauer, and the Belgian social democratic foreign minister, Paul-Henri Spaak.

They had expected progress to European Union to be far quicker and less problematic than has proved to be the case. The six founder members — Belgium, France, Holland, Italy, Luxembourg and West Germany — met at Messina in 1955 in the aftermath of the failure of the European Defence Community (EDC). The EDC had then been seen as the main hope of uniting Western Europe at a time of great tension in East–West relations.[3]

The EDC would have involved the active participation of a rearmed West Germany, and this was too much at the time for France, with bitter memories of the war and its traditional suspicion of the Germans. But the indifference of the British Conservative government also doomed the scheme. The consensus among politicians and military strategists in Britain was strongly opposed to any renewal of a military commitment 'on the continent'. This was in part a reflection of the traditional British preference for Naval power, and in part because of its wish to deploy a large proportion of its forces in colonial territories in Africa, Asia and the Caribbean. The British government also feared that outright commitment to a self-sufficient EDC might compromise the 'special relationship' with the United States, then in its first flush of illusory passion. Although the United States at that time was in favour of the EDC, as part of its strategy of 'containment' of the Soviet Union, British politicians were convinced that their influence in Washington was in direct proportion to their status as a world power. It was a delusion that would afflict Britain's European policy for some years.

Despite these setbacks the political tide in Western Europe was still running strongly towards greater unity. Frustrated by the collapse of the EDC, the six governments opted for a radically different strategy; laying the basis for political union by creating a common market. The unspoken assumption was that political unification would, more or less automatically, follow economic integration.

This optimism was kindled by the extraordinary world economic boom that lifted Western Europe during the 1950s and early 1960s. This prosperity shaped the character and ideals of the Treaty of Rome, which became the foundation charter and 'bible' of the EEC. During those years a full customs union was achieved, and at least the basis was laid for economic integration. Moreover the popular mood in those years was running strongly in favour of European supra-nationalism: memories of the last war were still vivid, and it was thought that only a united Europe could survive the threat to its independence posed by the Cold War division of the continent.

These illusions were rudely shattered in the constitutional row between France's President de Gaulle and the European Community in 1965. Although the crisis began with a conflict over the Community's powers to determine the annual budget, trouble had been brewing for some time. Indeed in his memoirs de Gaulle betrays his resentment of the supra-national pretensions of the Commission. Describing a visit to the then Commission President, Mr Walter Hallstein, de Gaulle says

(Hallstein) made Brussels . . . into a sort of capital. There he sat surrounded by all the trappings of sovereignty, directing his colleagues, allocating jobs among them, controlling several thousand officials . . . receiving the credentials of foreign ambassadors . . . concerned above all to further the amalgamation of the Six, believing the pressure of events would bring about what he envisaged.[3]

The confrontation between France and the Community was eventually resolved in January 1966, following discussions about the circumstances in which majority votes in the Council of Ministers should be deemed binding on individual countries. In essence this provided France, and any other government, with a right of veto in circumstances where it could claim that 'vital national interests' were affected by any decision of the Council. This so-called Luxembourg compromise blocked what had earlier been an evolution towards majority decisions and ensured that in subsequent years the EEC caravan moved at the pace of its slowest member.

Under the final agreement France agreed to reoccupy its seat at the Council of Ministers on condition that the Council could more closely scrutinize the Commission's budget, and that the credentials of non-member states accredited to the EEC would be received by the acting President of the Council and the Commission President, and not by the latter alone. The Commission promised to 'hold consultations with the Council . . . in a spirit of cooperation'.

Although the crisis over France's 'empty seat' at the Council of Ministers was defused, it left a mark on both the Commission and the overall decision-making processes of the Community. It defined the balance of power between the Community's decision-making institutions — the Commission, made up of politicians and civil servants appointed by the member states — and the Council of Ministers, consisting of ministers sent by each member government with the last say on policy decisions. The Commission never really recovered from the blow to its prestige and in the years that followed abandoned any serious belief that it was a 'European government in waiting'. However this belief reflected more than what General de Gaulle and others saw as the overweening ambitions of individual Commissioners. It also reflected the belief, widespread in the early years of the Community, that it would develop power and authority naturally, as member states agreed on new common policies to supersede national ones.

That is not to say that the Commission does not have important powers and an influential role. It is for the Commission, and not the Council to propose new policies, but while the Commission proposes the Council disposes, and because of that the Commission knows it has to operate within a consensus of member states.

In theory the Commission could attempt to appeal 'over the heads' of the national governments to European public opinion. This would not endear it to the governments, and few Commissions have ever mustered the courage to try such a course of action.

The power of the national governments is all the greater since it is they who appoint the Commission members and decide on extensions of their mandate. The large member states, in particular, seem to have a vested interest in appointing Commissioners who can be relied on not to rock the boat by asserting the 'European interest' too flagrantly against the Council. The result is that the kind of men (and it is invariably men) who get sent to Brussels are, in political terms, yesterday's men or never will be tomorrow's men. And the Commission is a comfortable posting: Commissioners are paid around £80,000 and retire with 75% of their salary.

The smaller countries benefit from the prestige of having an effective and influential EEC Commissioner. In recent years Pierre Lardinois (from Holland), Finn-Olav Gundelach (from Denmark) and Viscount Etienne Davignon (from Belgium) have come closer than most of their colleagues to being important international figures. Of recent Commission Presidents only Roy Jenkins (Britain) and Jacques Delors (France) have come to Brussels with a significant international reputation.

The Commission of course has a much wider role than merely proposing new policies. It is the guardian of the longer term goals and values enshrined in the Treaty of Rome, and does have significant management responsibility for areas like agriculture, competition policy, the steel industry and the customs union. These are among the areas where — for better or for worse — the Community has agreed on common policies. The Commission has a lesser though not unimportant role to play in regional and social development and high-tech research but it has only a marginal function in areas such as health and education, where the member states have strictly defined and limited the Community's supra-national 'competence'.

Even so the Community's rules on competition and its anti-monopoly legislation give the Commission wide powers of investigation into company practices. This is something directors never realize until the Commission's inspectors turn up at their head offices with authorization to enter and search at will.

As we shall see a little later, the emergence of the European Court of Justice as a semi-legislative body in its own right has given the Commission an occasionally powerful ally against the foot-dragging or malpractice of either government or private business. On more than one occasion the Commission and the European Parliament have threatened to bring national governments before the Court for not carrying out their duty, for instance to fix an annual budget large enough for the EEC to discharge its legal obligations.[4]

The Commission can, therefore, by no means be disregarded by national governments. Under its most recent President, Mr Jacques Delors, it has been readier than in the past to appeal to European public opinion to pressurize governments into a more enthusiastic commitment to the Community. Ironically the Commission has become a little more ready to risk the displeasure of the states in this way because it is aware that the European Parliament, frustrated at its own lack of power, might be tempted to use one of the very few sanctions in its constitutional armoury — and sack the entire Commission.

There is, however, a good case to be made for national governments not to appoint the members of the Commission (or at least its President) but for the European Parliament to do so. This would ensure more effective, if still indirect, accountability of the Commission to the European voter and it would also stiffen the political resolve of the Commission in its tussles with national governments. A more prestigious Commission, and one ready to assert its wider, supra-national, political authority, would also tend to attract a higher calibre of member.

There is also a sound case for reducing the number of Commission members — if only because there are not enough decent portfolios available for the current seventeen-person Commission, given the member states' tight grip on sovereignty. Matters are made more complicated by the fact that the larger member states (Britain, France, Italy, Spain and West Germany) are entitled to nominate two Commissioners while the others are entitled only to one.

A smaller, more efficient and more politically self-confident Commission could exercise more effective leadership of the Community at large. The lack of leadership has so far resulted in a political vacuum at the heart of the Community, with the blocking power of the Council of Ministers inadequately balanced by the Commission and European Parliament.

Like any large organization, the Commission has its bureaucratic strengths and weaknesses. It is expected to fill the more senior posts from among the twelve different nationalities, in predetermined — and jealously preserved — proportions. All too often that may mean filling a vacant post not with the best man or woman, but with the best available Briton, Luxembourger or Italian in the permanent European civil service.[5]

Sooner or later the twelve — or however many member states there then are in the Community — will have to scrap the national spoils system for filling key jobs in the Commission. This may also mean accepting a turnover system by which national officials spend a period in the European civil service without being expected to make it their lifetime careers or risking loss of seniority at home if they do take up posts for five or ten years in Brussels.

There are other problems. Something will have to be done about the 'Tower of Babel' of interpretation and translation but it is difficult to see quite what. It is only a matter of time before English joins French as the other 'working language' in the EEC institutions. In this respect the Commission has less of a problem than the European Parliament and some other bodies where interpretation into all nine 'official' languages is unavoidable, given the fact that so many MEPs are monolingual.

A further problem which afflicts all the EEC institutions is their geographical dispersal throughout the EEC, most notably in Brussels, Luxembourg and Strasbourg. Most Commission departments are to be found in Brussels in the Berlaymont building or in one of the many other satellite offices surrounding it in what is known as Brussels' 'Euro-quarter'. Other departments are housed in a similar area of Luxembourg city, which is also home

45

for the European Court of Justice, the European Investment Bank and the Secretariat of the European Parliament.

To complicate matters still further, the great majority of the plenary sessions of the European Parliament are held in Strasbourg, which prides itself on being the 'historic site of Franco–German reconciliation' and one of the spiritual homes of the idea of a united Europe. However, the key policy committees of the European Parliament normally meet in Brussels, while meetings of political groups and special inquiries can take place throughout the EEC. Strasbourg is also the site of the non-EEC Council of Europe, to which some twenty-one Western European states belong and which has its own occasional Parliamentary assemblies discussing questions of culture, education, health, and civil rights.

As a result of discussions in the Council of Europe, a European Convention on Human Rights was signed in 1950 under which violations of human rights are investigated by a Commission. Its findings can then be examined by the full European Court of Human Rights in Strasbourg.

While no one has suggested moving the Council of Europe or the Court of Human Rights, there is a powerful case for concentrating more of the EEC institutions in Brussels. A majority of European Parliamentarians are known to favour Brussels both for reasons of convenience and cost. The annual budget of the European Parliament is £220 million, and between one-third and one-half of this is attributable to the peculiar arrangement whereby the Parliament wanders between its present three sites. But there is also a political point. The European Parliament should be where the executives control which it does, or should already operate.

This logical conclusion is resisted both by the French masters of Strasbourg and by the Luxembourg government, both for reasons of prestige and because of the very considerable employment given by the EEC institutions in both cities. The Luxembourgers still insist that the Twelve honour a long-standing agreement to hold all meetings of the Council of Ministers in Luxembourg during three months of every year, even though this adds needlessly to the cost and complication of decision-making.

Both the Belgian and Luxembourg governments have also built

massive assembly buildings for the European Parliament in Brussels and Luxembourg city to rival the splendid — and expanded — Palace of Europe which currently houses the plenary sessions in Strasbourg. Someone, somewhere is going to have to call a halt to this kind of expensive nonsense. Considerations of sentiment apart, the logical answer is that the European Parliament and the Council should be restricted to Brussels, although there is no reason why the Court of Justice, the European Investment Bank and some Commission departments should not remain in Luxembourg. Strasbourg would still be left with the Council of Europe and the Court of Human Rights, both of which will continue to play a more prominent role in European affairs in the years ahead.

Ministers and Ambassadors

For all the attention that it receives, the European Commission is in terms of political power overshadowed by the Council of Ministers. The Council is the body that takes all the real policy decisions. Some of these take the form of regulations, which are compulsory and directly applicable to any member state, and some are directives. These are supposed to be binding but individual states are allowed to choose how to implement them.

Although legally there is only one Council of Ministers, for which the foreign ministers of the twelve member states are responsible, in practice there are many councils dealing with the different policy subjects such as the Finance Council, the Agriculture Council, the Transport Council, and so on.

There are in all a dozen different councils attended by the specialist ministers from the member states. All of them take decisions with the full authority of 'the Council', but in practice the meetings of foreign ministers act, or are meant to act, as a final court of appeal to resolve differences in lesser or specialist councils. But so serious in recent years have been the internal disagreements within the Community, notably over the reform of the Community's budget and its expenditure policies, that not even the foreign ministers have been able to resolve them. They have, in consequence, been referred even higher up: to the twice-annual meetings of the European Council.

47

The European Council is the name given to the summits of EEC heads of state and government. These meetings were never envisaged in the Treaty of Rome. But in 1974 the (then nine) member states of the EEC agreed, on the suggestion of the French President Giscard d'Estaing, that regular meetings at this level should deal with major world problems and their repercussions on the Community.[6]

Since then the European Council has become the ultimate court of appeal for the Council of Ministers, although their decisions are normally issued in the form of guidelines for the Council proper to implement. It was the European Council held in Copenhagen in 1978 that agreed the general lines of what later became the European Monetary System, while meetings held in Luxembourg in April 1980, London in December 1981 and Rambouillet in 1985, were dominated by crises over the budget and Britain's contribution to it. Over the years the Council's character has changed. It is less and less an informal exchange between heads of government about long-term global and strategic issues and much more a board of crisis management whose business is conducted in the full glare of media attention.

Reference has already been made to the national veto and the use of the precedent created by the Luxembourg compromise. Quite apart from their power of veto, which we have already described, the different members of the Council dispose of different numbers of votes, depending on their size. The number of votes cast by each national delegation is as follows: Belgium 5, Britain 10, Federal Republic of Germany 10, France 10, Greece 5, Ireland 3, Italy 10, Luxembourg 2, Netherlands 5, Portugal 5, and Spain 10. As we have seen, some decisions have to be on the basis of unanimity but an increasing number, since the adoption of the Single European Act, can be by 'qualified majority', that is, a total of fifty-three votes. Therefore it only takes two larger member states allied with one small country to block a move supported by the other nine states, who have between them a simple majority of votes.[7]

This form of veto has played a crucial role in the in-fighting between different countries over fixing not only the overall size of the Community budget, but the amount of money to be devoted to specific items, since votes are taken line by line covering all the detailed spending commitments in the budget.

None of the ministers concerned with EEC affairs is, of course, based in Brussels and so they have to travel from national capitals for meetings of the Council. But they are advised by perhaps the least well known, and in some ways most influential decision-making body in the Community, the Committee of Permanent Representatives (or ambassadors) which looks after the interests of the twelve member governments between meetings of the full European Council.

The committee is popularly known by its French acronym COREPER. It was set up when the EEC Commission, the European Coal and Steel Community (which had preceded the establishment of the EEC) and the European Atomic Energy Community (Euratom) were merged in July 1967. This treaty also established a single Parliamentary assembly, a common Court of Justice and a united economic and social committee.

One unusual feature of the permanent representations of the member states in Brussels, by comparison with most foreign embassies, is that they are staffed not only by career diplomats but by civil servants representing domestic government departments. This is necessary because of the volume of domestic legislation now directly or indirectly affected by what is decided in Brussels.

It would not be entirely accurate however, to compare COREPER and its specialist offshoot committees with the way in which the government machine operates nationally. While it is true that those serving on COREPER operate under national policy guidelines laid down by the politicians at home, officials in Brussels do have far wider latitude to interpret the 'national interest' than would be typical in most national capitals. This inevitably raises questions of democratic accountability and of the public 'transparency' of the EEC's complex decision-making process. But the issue of democratic accountability goes even deeper.

For it is the Council of Ministers rather than the European Assembly in Strasbourg that is the closest to a proper Parliament, in the sense that it is the Council which enacts laws. It does so, however, behind closed doors. Its decisions are subject only to a questionably effective form of surveillance and control by national Parliaments. National Parliamentary control of the Council of Ministers is completely inadequate; because national Parliaments are generally so ill-informed about what goes on in Brussels, because of the inherent complexity of the issues, and because MPs cannot directly mandate ministers who go to Brussels.

The exception is the Danish Parliament, or *Folketing*, whose European Community sub-committee is able to lay down broad mandates that have to be observed by Danish ministers who attend Council meetings. It is not unknown for Danish ministers at a Council meeting to have to ask for a suspension of business to enable them to check with the chair of the European Community *Folketing* committee that a decision is in line with agreed policy. This irritates other EEC governments, who do not operate under the same restraints. (The peculiar authority of the *Folketing* committee owes much to the parliamentary situation in Denmark in which minority coalition government's must frequently deal with assemblies controlled by the opposition.)

The Council is both a forum for multilateral or intergovernmental negotiations, where it is perfectly normal to expect deliberations to be private, as well as a body that passes laws for the 180 million people of the European Community. But why should this aspect of the Council's offices be conducted in secret?

Mr Tony Benn, when Secretary of State for Industry, did raise this question and suggested that the Council be opened up to the public when it passes laws. There were no takers for this novel idea. More remarkably, the European Parliament itself is not associated with the decisions of the Council, except in determining the annual budget, presumably for fear that MEPs would use such privileged access to get their hands on greater power.

The Toothless Parliament

The European Parliament was, from the start, seen as an integral part of the European Community, and was directly referred to in the treaties establishing the EEC. Until 1979, when the first direct elections were held, the European Parliament consisted of nominated members of the national Parliaments. The nominated Parliament was hardly less effective than its directly elected successor has since proved to be.

Under the foundation treaties of the Community, the Council of Ministers is obliged to consult the Parliament on a wide range of legislative matters and this has actually been increased as a result of the Single European Act. However the Parliament has very few powers it can invoke to get its way when it wishes to 'comment' on such matters. It can merely delay its 'advice' in ways that can upset the Council's decision-makimg timetable, in order to influence the final outcome.

The one exception to this pattern of impotence is the fixing of the annual budget. This the European Parliament can reject in its entirety. Apart from that MEPs have only a very limited capacity to amend the rate of increase of 'non-obligatory' expenditure. This means, for example, that MEPs cannot themselves reduce spending on the Common Agricultural Policy, since this is deemed 'obligatory' under EEC rules. Even where the assembly moves to increase spending on 'non-obligatory' policies, such as research or regional and social development, the actual amount of cash at its disposal is minimal and the rate of growth permitted from year to year is determined restrictively by what is known as the 'maximum rate' formula.

The European Parliament has won the right to question the ministerial representative of whatever country is filling the EEC Presidency (each country having a six-month turn at the helm of EEC affairs). As we have seen, the Parliament cannot mandate or sanction the Council, but that does not prevent MEPs debating all the issues that come before ministers and attempting to win public support for their views.

Even as a debating chamber, however, the European Parliament has not been notably effective. More often than not MEPs are divided, not by ideology or political belief, but nationally. The unpredictable outcome of votes is exacerbated by the MEP's poor record of actual attendance at debates in Strasbourg.[8] Successive Presidents of the European Parliament, who are elected every two-and-a-half years, have complained how difficult it is to secure a quorum at the end of the week during plenary sessions of the assembly in Strasbourg.

This has, more than once, led the assembly to reach conflicting and even blatantly contradictory conclusions. This has occurred for instance, in the one area where the MEPs have limited powers — the annual budget. Parliament was quite capable of voting for both tough curbs on spending and against any limit on CAP expenditure.

Even where Euro-Parliamentarians do reach a clear consensus, for instance in support of greater resources for research, industrial development, or regional and social expenditure the Council has frequently ignored them and cut spending lines devoted to these subjects. And when it comes to the one sanction the Parliament does dispose of — outright rejection of the budget — there has rarely been a majority for action.

The Parliament can also sack the entire EEC Commission. But the Commission rarely gives the Parliament cause for that degree of discontent; indeed the Commission is often on the same side as the European Parliament against the Council of Ministers. If power really corrupts, and absolute power corrupts absolutely, having precious little power is equally corrupting. The trouble with the European Parliament is that it is not a 'Parliament' in the proper sense of the word. It does not legislate: it is merely a consultative assembly.

Why, it might be asked, go to all the trouble of electing a European Parliament only to exclude it from any real share in power? That question seems to have occurred to many of the European Community's voters. This may explain why the turnout in the two European elections held to date has been so disappointing.

In the last direct elections in 1984, the turnout of voters throughout the Community fell to 57 per cent compared with 61 per cent in the first such election, held in 1979. Actually if account is taken of countries where voting is compulsory — Belgium, Greece, Italy and Luxembourg — the true fall in turnout was nearer 7 per cent. The UK had the lowest voting figure of any EEC country, with a turnout of just 32 per cent — well below the average for local elections or even for the referendum on

Community membership held in 1975. According to work done by 'Eurobarometer' this reflected a low awareness of the role and significance of the Parliament, as much as any residual British hostility to the Community, which polls show to have been on the decline since British accession to the EEC in 1973.

In countries with a well-established interest in European affairs, like Italy (where many politicians openly support a united federal Europe), the turnout has been reasonably high. At the other end of the spectrum, in Britain, the voters were completely indifferent and there were even some polling districts in 1986 where no one voted at all.

Britain is by no means the only country where electors do not know the name of their MEP. Very few politicians have managed to make a name for themselves in Strasbourg, and the few that have, have normally been eager to swap their European mandate for the chance to contest an election to their national Parliament.

This is in spite of extraordinarily generous pay and conditions. A British MEP, for example, is paid around £20,000 (the same rate as Westminster), but can claim allowances for secretaries and researchers, and travelling and other expenses that can take his or her annual pay nearer to £50,000. The temptation in these circumstances to accept political marginality, and enjoy a life of high-class political tourism is too great for some members. Involvement of most members in the laborious work of the European Parliament's committees is poor and there are episodic scandals over the MEPs' abuse of expenses.

This is encouraged by the lax rules for the payment of expenses for members attending meetings, not primarily in Brussels (where most committee meetings are held) or Strasbourg (the site of the Parliament's plenary sessions) but elsewhere in the Community. Political group meetings can occur anywhere in Europe, as can so-called 'study days' where MEPs gather to discuss the problems of specific regions. In addition the Parliament sends a large number of delegations to other countries, including other Parliamentary bodies. It is all too easy for MEPs to register their attendance on these occasions; there is virtually no check on their active participation. This author has been told by some MEPs that they can add to their generous salaries another third by such means.

When the founders of the European Community conceived the idea of a directly elected Parliament they did so because they believed that by the time direct elections came to pass, a powerful, supra-national European executive — an embryo European government — would have evolved, probably by the late 1970s. This point was put to me very strongly by the former Federal German Chancellor, Willy Brandt, who did not disguise his concern at the European Parliament's loss of credibility as an institution, as a result of its highly restricted powers. The founders recognized that without being given a proper democratic mandate through direct elections, the European Parliament would be in no position to control a European executive.

The European government did not evolve beyond the embryo. The concentration of power at a European level has been slower and much more fitful than seemed possible in 1957. Some have concluded that there is no need to give the European Parliament a bigger political role until much more executive power has been transferred from the national governments to the Community. But this ignores the real, if veiled, power the Council of Ministers already exercises.

The European Parliament should therefore be given greater power. It should appoint members of the Commission and should have the right to replace individual Commissioners, not just the whole team at once. The Council should be made much more answerable to the Parliament for its decisions. It would help if MEPs could, as of right, participate in the national Parliament's EEC vetting committees. Above all the MEPs should be given far greater power to amend the annual budget, not just the relatively small sums devoted to non-agricultural expenditure.

None of these steps by themselves would necessarily transform the European Parliament, but with some real power to be fought for, the different political groups in the assembly would have to organize themselves more effectively and give a greater priority to campaigns on shared political programmes. It might even result in a better calibre of member becoming interested in the European

Parliament, to say nothing of counteracting the massive indifference of voters to it.

The 1984 election produced a Parliament where no party enjoyed an overall majority. The socialists emerged as the largest group with 130 members followed by the European People's Party (Christian Democrats) with 110 members, European Democratic Group (mainly British Conservatives) with fifty members, forty-one communists, thirty-one Liberals, European Progressive Democrats (mainly French Gaullists and Irish Fianna Fail MEPs) with twenty-nine members, the Rainbow Group (mainly radical Green MEPs) with twenty members, sixteen neo-fascists and seven independent members. Since the accession of Portugal and Spain in 1986, MEPs have been appointed to swell the numbers of some of these groups but their relative strengths have not changed. Both countries will participate in the next direct elections in June 1989.

In the case of Britain, the best-known MEP probably remains the former leader of the British Labour Group — which is at times an uneasy constituent of the wider European Parliament Socialist Group — Mrs Barbara Castle. This, however, is more a tribute to her former career as a national politician and minister in Harold Wilson's governments during the 1960s than to her role in the European Parliament. Others, such as the Reverend Ian Paisley, the Ulster Protestant Unionist leader, hit the headlines from time to time. He is a specialist in disruptive demonstrations in the Strasbourg Assembly when it is addressed by Southern Irish government leaders. Despite their relative inexperience, a lot of hard work is done by MEPs working on specialist committees of the Parliament. Inevitably, MEPs who partake actively in this work develop an expertise on Community affairs not found in national Parliaments. This is one good reason why European Community select committees at Westminster should coopt British MEPs, even as non-voting members, to give themselves a degree of expertise. In the longer run, however, the standing and impact of the European Parliament will decline unless it is given greater powers and responsibility in EEC decision making. The longer this is delayed, the greater is the danger that the European Parliament will be stuck with its public image of irrelevance, which

55

would make it even more difficult for the assembly to be given the powers it needs.

Courts and Committees

No survey of the political geography of the Community can focus solely on the Council, the Commission and the Parliament. There are other official and semi-official bodies whose role is crucial in determining the pattern of EEC policy making.

The European Court of Justice consists of thirteen members with the status of judges appointed by the twelve member states, and seven Advocates General, whose function is to give the court advisory opinions on the merits of the cases which come before them. It is the Court's function both to interpret Community law, where that is contested, and also to hear cases of alleged breaches of European regulations, whether by private bodies or state authorities. The volume of cases coming before the Court has expanded in recent years, partly because of the steady growth in European legislation passed by the Council, and partly because of complex disputes involving national governments. On occasions, one European institution takes another to the Court. In this sense the Court, unlike British courts, has a quasi-political function. The Court's rulings on subjects as diverse as women's right to equal pay for equal work, two-tier pricing of cars by the British on the Continent and in the UK, on German efforts to defend the purity of their beer and on the right of women in the Royal Ulster Constabulary to carry guns, have had a direct influence on the general public.[10]

The UK appears to have one of the worst records for alleged breaches of the Treaty of Rome, but more and more cases are being instigated not by the Commission but by private individuals against their own governments. A similar trend is evident in appeals to the non-EEC European Court of Human Rights in Strasbourg. The Court of Human Rights has upheld appeals by British parents against the use of corporal punishment in schools and, in 1977, upheld an appeal by the *Sunday Times* in the famous Thalidomide case. At the time of writing it is considering appeals against the British government's ban on the publication of the memoirs of a former member of the British security services.

Some legal experts deplore the fact that, for the first time in British history, even the highest courts in the land have to bow to the judgement of a superior court overseas. On the other hand the existence of both the European Courts has undoubtedly increased the scope for individuals and social groups to challenge the bureaucratic fiat of the national state.

An institution that lies in the no-man's-land between the official and the unofficial is the Economic and Social Committee which has functioned in Brussels since 1958. It is made up of employers' organizations, trade unions and 'special interests', such as agricultural, consumer, commercial and professional organizations appointed by the relevant national federations in each member state. The committee currently has some 200 members who meet each month to give their formal advice on a wide range of social and commercial policy directives on their way from the Commission to the Council of Ministers. It is able only to 'advise', however, and has no powers to amend or reject proposed legislation.

Within the Economic and Social Committee a crucial role is played by the employers' organization in the EEC (known by its French acronym UNICE) by the European Trade Union Confederation (ETUC) representing the different trade union congresses, and the most powerful farmers' lobby, known by its acronym COPA.

In recent years the power of the trade unions and the farmers' organizations has diminished somewhat. This is partly because tripartite policy making between the so-called 'social partners' (government, unions and employers) has gone out of fashion in EEC countries. But the decline in the power of COPA is a direct consequence of the years of intense crisis in European farming which is now leading to a radical reform in the system of high and guaranteed prices for farm output.

On the other hand, a body far less well known to the European public, which has no official standing in Brussels, but which is playing an ever more influential role, is the European Round

Table. It consists of some of the most senior executives in the most powerful of Western Europe's multinational corporations

The Round Table organization was established by a Swede, Mr Pehr Gyllenhammar, the chairman of Volvo, in 1983 as a sort of club of leading industrialists 'to strengthen and develop Europe's industrial base'. This is to be achieved by promoting trans-national business and cooperation between major European companies. From its inception a key role has been played in the European Round Table by the former EEC Industry Commissioner, Viscount Etienne Davignon, who has long espoused the cause of greater European corporate integration. The Round Table is a lobby for policies that will facilitate the emergence of a single European market, big enough and free enough to permit the growth of European multinationals sufficiently large and technologically advanced to face intensifying competition from American and Japanese corporations.[11]

The combination of the Round Table's discreet influence with the political dominance of free-trade and right-wing governments in Europe has been a potent one in recent years. It is responsible for putting the completion of the internal market and the free movement of capital and trade at the top of the Community's political agenda. The reverse side of this coin is the decline in influence of what might be called the European social-democratic project. Policies of social reform, including measures to strengthen the consultative rights of organized labour or to curb the activities of multinationals, are out of fashion.

It remains to be seen whether the political pendulum swings back to the left in the 1990s. If it does this will lead to a new set of priorities for the EEC. For the moment it is capital and big business which is setting the agenda and giving direction and coherence to the policies of the European institutions.

3
Atlantic Divorce

It has been observed that if the European Community existed on the moon, it would have fallen apart long ago. In other words, what binds the different states of the EEC together is pressure from the external world rather than an automatic or permanent community of interest. The national states of the EEC hang together, lest they be hanged separately.

The point can be overstated. The longer the European Community survives and the more accustomed its citizens become to living and working within an evolving framework of collective government, the less likely it will be that any member country will revert to national isolation.

The challenges of an increasingly competitive external world nevertheless provide much of the incentive for European cooperation. There is nothing new in that. The world economic system has long been driven by a competitive compulsion to accumulate, to innovate, to control new markets and to overcome rivals. What has changed is the scale and intensity of international competition, which, in one form or another, now dominates economic activity in all but the most underdeveloped and remote areas of the world.

The past thirty years have seen an extraordinary expansion not only in world trade, but also in the deployment of international finance and, more recently, of new forms of international production. The imperative to compete internationally increasingly determines national economic priorities. The world-wide network of currency and capital markets, whose volume and speed of transactions have been further revolutionized by the computer and international telecommunications, act as an effective means of monitoring and disciplining errant national economies.

Under modern conditions it is more and more difficult for any one economy to 'buck the international trend'. During a period when countries throughout the industrialized world have pursued policies of economic deflation, monetarism, and industrial restructuring, governments attempting to move in the opposite direction have discovered what it means to forfeit the confidence of the international financial markets.

This was the experience of the French socialist-communist coalition in the early 1980s, and of Mr Papandreou's PASOK (Pan-Hellenic Socialist Movement) regime in Greece a few years later, when they attempted to pursue expansionist, neo-Keynesian economic policies. In the end they were forced to reverse direction and impose the kind of austerity policies favoured by the international capital markets.[1]

Meanwhile, even more onerous sacrifices are demanded of the debt-burdened economies of many developing countries, when they apply for new loans. One of the very few countries able to run massive balance of payments deficits and to require the rest of the world to finance its internal spending programmes has been the United States. As we shall see, the special immunity of the United States to the punitive and costly economic adjustments typically demanded by the International Monetary Fund has been bought by the privileged status of the dollar as the world's main reserve asset and international trading currency.

Yet even the might of the US economy may not be enough to ensure continued immunity. The day has been drawing closer when the rest of the world will refuse to fund the US deficits unless the American government accepts the necessity of a painful domestic economic restructuring. That was the message of the stock market crash of October 1987.

The sinews binding the world economy together are more numerous than the strands of international trade and finance, crucial though these are. Production itself is becoming internationalized. Typically, large, multinational corporations control most of the different elements of an interdependent production process, including diversified research and development, even when these are located in several different countries.

In an impressive account of this development, Robin Murray

cites the case of Ford UK, which until the late 1960s relied on a manufacturing network within Britain, including its own engine workshops, body plants, and foundries.[2] Today Ford UK supplies diesel engines to Ford Europe and imports petrol engines from Valencia. The Fiesta, which is assembled at Dagenham, uses transmission systems made in Bordeaux, wheels from Genk in Belgium, body panels from Spain and suspension components from Ford of West Germany.

This is but one dramatic instance of a global phenomenon in manufacturing industry. The large multinationals today have — in Murray's words — 'consolidated around the supply of primary product technology, of advanced management systems, of international marketing and/or have developed synthetic substitutes which can be produced in first world factories rather than on third world land'.

A similar process is under way in retailing. Marketing in many different countries is undertaken with the aid of computers, and supplies are obtained from a wide range of firms in different countries. Murray notes that 'subcontracting and franchising are two rapidly growing expressions of capitalism's new era of "flexible specialization" '.

The consequences of these developments for national economic and industrial policies are only beginning to be understood. For instance it is becoming clear that 'nationalization' of one component of the integrated manufacturing system of a large multinational can be rendered ineffective in terms of control of investment, production or innovation. Effective foreign exchange control also poses immense problems in an era of transfer pricing by multinationals from one national subsidiary to another, international banking integration and capital liberalization, coupled with the systematic policy within the EEC of outlawing national subsidies and industrial controls. The result is the effective dismantling of the conventional armoury of national economic intervention employed in the past by left or Keynesian governments.

This is one factor forcing political parties of all persuasions to think increasingly in European terms. For the right this means encouraging the process of liberalization and the development of a Europe-wide market. The left is less clear about its reaction: it may involve a new form of democratic planning at a European level, and new forms of supra-national economic intervention and public ownership. Demands are already coming from the labour movement and other social groups for the 'harmonization' of economic, social and other benefits and rights within a European framework.[3]

The very success of business and finance in creating a 'European dimension' is now finding an echo in demands for a 'Social Europe'. There is fertile ground for development in social welfare standards, civil and trade union rights, taxation and measures for increased industrial democracy.

It would be wrong, however, to see the internationalization of the economic system as external to the political structures of the state. Global growth in manufacturing productivity has immensely exacerbated imbalances in trade flows between different parts of national economies, as well as reinforcing long-term disparities in technological innovation and, more broadly, in competitiveness. These developments pose highly political problems for national states.

The experience of the past ten to fifteen years of alternating bouts of inflationary growth and recession, combined with the steady shift of traditional manufacturing industries from the older industrialized economies in Western Europe and North America to the newly industrialized countries of the Pacific Rim and, to a degree, Latin America, have inflamed international economic and trade tensions. The international system seems to be coagulating into global trading and financial regions.

The United States, of course, remains the core and political centre of one such region. Following its free trade agreement with the United States in 1987, Canada may become an uncertain junior partner, with a variety of Latin American client state economies in reluctant tow. Despite the protracted decline in its international value, the US dollar remains the region's currency linchpin.

Across the Pacific another region appears to be in the making, centred economically, if not yet politically, on Japan. Such a region would include the Newly Industrialized Countries such as

South Korea, Taiwan and some of the member states of the Association of South East Asian Nations (ASEAN). In spite of the impressive economic power of this region, it still lacks elementary political coherence, not least because of deep-seated historical objections to any suggestion of Japanese political or security hegemony.

Clearly there is still a 'Soviet bloc', although as we shall see later it is in the grip of a thoroughgoing economic and political crisis. One key aspect of this crisis is the growing detachment of some East European former 'satellite' states from the direct control of the Soviet Union. Some states in Eastern Europe may find themselves drawn into a process leading to the reunification of the European region.

There are a number of aspirant global regions. China seeks to be one, although it may not be able to sustain the development pattern needed to prevent subordination to some other, more global economic power. This is even more true for those Middle Eastern oil states and Andean or other South American countries who are seeking to become significant regional groupings.

The significance of this regionalization process should not be exaggerated. The non-communist industrialized countries still identify with the international economic order laid down under American auspices at the end of the Second World War. Though their prestige and effectiveness have declined, the International Monetary Fund, the General Agreement on Tariffs and Trade, the Organization for Economic Cooperation and Development and the other institutions of the post-war 'Atlantic order' still function and seek to preserve a relatively open, 'liberal' global economic order.

Nevertheless, the last ten years have seen the unmistakable erosion of this post-war system, undermined by the decline in American economic and political power since the late 1960s. Nowhere is this more striking than in the evolution of the Europe–US relationship, which is now approaching something of a crisis.

Transatlantic conflict has arisen over economic policy, trade, foreign policy goals, and even over defence and security arrangements. Probably no other single development will shape the future of the European Community over the next ten years as decisively as this gradual unravelling of the 'Atlantic partnership'.

The origin of these tensions is complex. It has something to do with the fact that since the mid-1960s the European Community countries have gained on the United States in productive economic power and overtaken it as a world trade power. Then there is the disruptive impact on the European economies of the decline of the US dollar as a non-inflationary store of value and reserve currency asset.

There are deep-seated differences of perspective about world problems whose origins lie further back in history, but which were largely sublimated on the European side in the immediate post-war years when Western European states felt themselves dependent on American economic and military support. Transatlantic rivalries have been intensified by the struggle for world markets which has characterized relations between all the major Western economic powers since the mid-1970s.[4]

Most writers on the subject now agree that the transatlantic relationship started to turn sour in 1973, ironically chosen by President Nixon and his Secretary of State, Henry Kissinger, as the 'Year of Europe'. The deteriorating state of the US economy, notably the deficit in the US trade balance, was already giving cause for alarm. The Nixon Administration tried to stimulate unilateral economic action to restore US fortunes by breaking the link between the dollar and gold.[5]

The effect was to devalue the dollar against the currencies of its main Atlantic partners, and thus to weaken confidence in the dollar as the primary store of value for corporate and governmental savings in the international monetary system. In the years that followed, successive US Administrations, in the eyes of European governments, exercised a policy of 'benign neglect' of the dollar. The former West German Chancellor, Helmut Schmidt, spoke in the mid-1970s of the 'misuse of the dollar as an instrument of US foreign policy'.

Worse, the US budget and balance of trade deficits steadily deteriorated during the Ford, Carter and Reagan years. One result of a dollar-based world financial system was that Europe (and subsequently Japan especially) ended up financing America's overspending because they were obliged to accumulate dollar assets in settlement of America's debts.

By the mid-1980s there were real fears in Europe that the entire international monetary system could be imperilled by the continuing US deficits. Paradoxically, the sheer scale of the US deficits had helped the world economy stage a partial recovery from the recessions of the early 1970s and early 1980s, but by 1987 the possibility existed that the inability of the United States to continue financing its deficits might plunge the world into an outright economic depression.

Worse still, it was feared, the deficits might lead to such an increase in international interest rates by the end of the decade that some of the Third World countries with the greatest indebtedness to Western banks would be obliged to default on their debt repayments. That, in turn, could lead to the doomsday scenario: a series of international banking crashes turning economic recession into a slump comparable with the 1930s. The stock market crash of October 1987 seemed to confirm the worst apprehensions of the West European governments.

Through the 1970s and increasingly in the 1980s, the United States and the European Community found themselves on a collision course over international trade. In part this was due to the effects of recession and more intense competition for international export markets. But friction was exacerbated by increasing trade protectionism. By the late 1970s there were doubts whether the GATT system of international free trade could survive for long.

During the 1970s, for example, the United States had sought to protect its battered steel industry, hit at that time by a temporarily inflated dollar, through a system of trigger prices designed to ward off European and Japanese competition. Europe also accused the United States of deliberately underpricing its oil, despite the world-wide crisis triggered by the 1973 OPEC oil price increase, in order to help American chemical and synthetic textile manufacturers undercut foreign competition.

On the other hand the Americans charged the Europeans with using massive government subsidies to aid some of their industries — not only sectors hit by the international crisis, such as steel, shipbuilding and textiles, but also the aircraft industry. This row came to a head in 1987 with US threats against the European Airbus.

There is no doubt that the European Community, and more especially its member states, made aggressive use of state subsidies both to protect threatened industries and to help launch new, high-tech sectors to challenge American and Japanese dominance. But for their part the Europeans could, with equal justice, point out that the United States had long used its defence and armaments research and development as an indirect subsidy to the industries concerned.[6]

Thus when the United States announced in 1985 that it would spend billions of dollars to research and develop its Strategic Defence Initiative the European states complained that this would give a massive indirect boost to America's advanced information technologies, reinforcing Europe's relative technological backwardness and consequent dependence on the United States.

The EEC reaction to these developments was to intensify the search for greater European self-sufficiency. The EUREKA project, initiated by industrialists in both the EEC and EFTA, and, more specifically, European Community technology programmes such as ESPRIT, BRITE and RACE involved a collective commitment to research and development. They are the direct offspring of this European determination not to be subordinated to US or Japanese technology.

Serious though these industrial and technological rivalries have been, they have been dwarfed by the agricultural trade war. On several occasions in the past few years the EEC and the US have come close to introducing sweeping sanctions against each other's exports because of bitter disagreements over farm trade questions. There have even been warnings from leaders on both sides that, left unresolved, these conflicts could poison the political basis of the Atlantic Alliance. At first sight this appears to be gross exaggeration but there has always been a link between transatlantic consensus on global economic and commercial questions and the commitment of the United States to the costly 'defence' of Western Europe.[7]

'It is not right, proper or wise for the United States to make decisions about keeping troops in Europe on the basis of whether the Common Market treats soyabeans fairly,' Henry Kissinger observed as long ago as 1973. 'But there is no way to prevent [this]. The political, military and economic issues in Atlantic relations are linked by reality, not by choice, nor for the tactical purpose of trading one off against the other.'

The most outrageous aspect of the CAP, from the American standpoint, is not the direct subsidies paid to producers: since total government support for American farmers — at around $26 billion a year — is greater than the £20 billion figure in the EEC, while state support for Japanese farmers — about $50 billion — exceeds the US and EEC totals combined. What upsets the American and, it must be said, many other food exporting nations is the system of export subsidies paid to enable the Common Market to dispose of part of its massive surpluses of food on world markets.

The precipitate decline in the value of the dollar — in which world food prices are calculated — combined with much lower production costs outside the EEC have resulted in the payment of massive subsidies to bridge the gap between world and European farm prices. The principal losers have been the farmers in developing countries whose markets have been undermined by the dumping of cheap European food. But the use of subsidies has heightened competition between the EEC and the US for key agricultural export markets in areas such as the Middle East, North Africa and elsewhere. Indeed conflict over whether or not Eygpt was a 'traditional' American or European market for grain very nearly became a commercial *casus belli* in the early 1980s.

To make matters worse the system of import levies protecting European farmers from foreign imports and the expansion of the EEC to embrace Portugal and Spain, which had been important markets for American animal feedstuffs, provided another flashpoint in Euro–American trade relations in 1987. But the most serious US threat of all-out trade conflict came, in the same year, when the EEC Commission proposed a tax on vegetable oils and fats which, if adopted by the twelve, would have severely damaged US exports of soyabeans.

Transatlantic suspicions and recriminations seem certain to intensify if the US Congress adopts any significant part of the highly protectionist Trade Bill which was being considered at the end of 1987. In the view of EEC experts, some of the proposals being put to the Reagan Administration threaten swingeing controls on imports of a wide range of different products, with serious consequences for exports from the European Community.

The growing trade conflict between the United States and Japan has hardly reassured European observers. EEC leaders were alarmed when, in 1987, the US and Japanese governments negotiated a series of 'voluntary restraint' agreements designed to reduce Japanese shipments to the US and thus the deficit in US trade with Japan, which was running at around $50 billion a year. The European Commission feared that such bilateral trade deals could lead to a 'tidal wave' of Japanese exports diverted from the American to the European Community market.

Given these intertwined issues of finance and trade, international intervention will be required to forestall a trade war, and much will depend on the new round of trade liberalization negotiations within GATT. The probability of a new world recession in 1988 or 1989 makes a successful outcome unlikely.

Transatlantic trade conflict has been, on occasions, overtly 'political'. A striking case in point was the move in 1982 by the United States to impose sanctions against European companies which had tendered successfully for Soviet contracts to build an oil pipeline between Siberia and Western Europe. The hawkish Reagan Administration viewed the contract as a violation of rules agreed within NATO to restrict exports of high technology goods of potential strategic importance to the Soviet military effort.

Indeed the rulings by COCOM, a committee of NATO governments set up to vet 'sensitive' high technology exports to the Soviet Union, have frequently led to bitter objections by West European firms and governments. The suspicion in Europe has been that COCOM controls have sometimes not been justified on grounds of security but have been imposed for ideological reasons and to discourage the opening up of the Soviet market by European business interests.[8]

As West European industry tries to open up the markets of the Soviet bloc countries, and especially if it responds to invitations by the Soviet state bodies, there is bound to be conflict over how to interpret COCOM rules. Europe's high technology expertise will continue to attract the Soviet authorities to these joint ventures.

Politics, some philosophers have claimed, is merely a matter of 'concentrated economics'. Be that as it may, there has been a clear divergence of political perceptions between Western Europe and the United States in recent years, although shared membership of the Atlantic Alliance, and the coincidence of right-wing trends on both sides of the Atlantic in the 1980s has helped to contain these differences.

Even so, there has been a remarkable decline in the standing of the United States in the eyes of its European allies. Opinion polls carried out prior to the negotiations to eliminate medium-range nuclear forces in Europe made dismal reading in Washington. They revealed that people in Western Europe increasingly blame the United States more than the Soviet Union for tensions in super-power relations and see the United States as less committed to disarmament than its rival. A poll commissioned by the US Information Agency in November 1986 showed that 43 per cent of West Germans blamed the United States for the failure of the Reykjavik summit that year against only 6 per cent who blamed Moscow. A British TV poll showed that a remarkable 49 per cent of British people now believed that the UK's 'special relationship' with the US was 'harmful' against 39 per cent who thought it 'helpful'.[9]

This growing mood of opposition to the United States and its policies has greatly worried its NATO partners. But they have had their own conflicts with Washington, most notably over lack of consultation prior to the opening of the INF negotiations. Some European governments fear that the signing in December 1987 of the Soviet–American INF agreement heralds the 'denuclearization' of Western Europe and the 'uncoupling' of the United States from the defence of the region. The agreement, which abolishes medium-range, land-based nuclear missiles, was a landmark in East–West relations. But its impact on the way Europeans think about their own defence and security was at least as great.

European attitudes to defence, and specifically nuclear defence, have constituted the most controversial single issue in domestic politics since the late 1960s. Public opinion polarized after the development of what has been described as the 'Second Cold War' between the nuclear super-powers from the late 1970s and in particular, the decision by NATO to deploy some 570 Cruise and Pershing 2 medium-range nuclear missiles in Western Europe after 1979. For some, this was a correct response to the development of new missile systems by the Warsaw Pact countries, notably the Soviet SS20 missiles. The European governments who persuaded a reluctant United States to deploy the missiles believed that the integrity of NATO's doctrine of 'flexible response' to a perceived Soviet military threat was at stake.

To many other Europeans, the deployment of the missiles — together with the parallel and unprecedented build-up of America's overall nuclear arsenal by the Reagan Administration — threatened a new and far more dangerous phase in the arms race. The early 1980s witnessed an extraordinary upsurge in the popularity and radicalism of the European peace movement, with monster demonstrations in virtually all West European countries and notably in the five 'host' states — Belgium, Britain, Holland, Italy and West Germany.

The scale of public opposition to the new nuclear front and other aspects of NATO's deterrence strategies led, indirectly, to a moderation of the new policies. As a result, the United States offered to negotiate not just a reduction in the Cruise and Pershing missiles but their entire abolition, providing the SS20 missiles were withdrawn as well.

Subsequently the US supreme military commander of NATO, General Bernard Rogers, criticized this decision: Western powers had, he said, bowed to the pressure of the peace movement without really believing that the Soviet Union would ever agree to negotiate the abolition of their SS20 missiles.[10] In the event, the emergence of Mikhail Gorbachev in 1985 was followed by a remarkable evolution in official Soviet policy on nuclear arms control. In 1987 one NATO expert said that in the previous two years — prior to the signing of the INF agreement — there had been 'twenty-five largely unilateral and unreciprocated major "moves" or "shifts", by the Soviet Secretary General Mikhail

Gorbachev, towards the United States in arms control diplomacy.'[11]

Not only did Gorbachev accept the notion of a 'zero option' agreement abolishing medium-range missiles but he offered a 'double zero' agreement by including a sub-category of short-range missiles. The resulting agreement removed all medium- and short-range ground-launched missiles — that is those with a range of between 500 and 5500 kilometres — and promised their destruction in the five years that would follow US Congressional endorsement of the agreement in the summer of 1988.

The speed with which the agreement was negotiated and signed by the leaders of the United States and the Soviet Union took European public opinion by surprise. Supporters of the decision to deploy Cruise and Pershing missiles immediately claimed the credit, arguing that their tough stand had forced the Soviet government to the negotiating table.[12] With equal alacrity, the Western European peace movement claimed a victory in its campaign of popular pressure against nuclear weapons on European soil. Other goals remained: the abolition of all other nuclear weapons, starting with battlefield systems; a maximum reduction in conventional arms; and the liquidation of both NATO and the Warsaw Pact.[13]

The reaction of most European NATO governments was altogether more cautious. Indeed, they displayed a marked lack of enthusiasm when the prospect of an INF agreement first emerged. The speed with which the United States was willing to negotiate away weapons originally deployed under Western European pressure was seen as further disturbing evidence of a growing gap between American and West European perceptions of their security interests.

In the end the European NATO states were persuaded by Washington to welcome the agreement, aware that it was a *fait accompli* and popular with their own peoples. But the United States was warned not to press ahead with further agreements on other nuclear weapons systems which might lead to the 'denuclearization' of NATO's strategy in Europe.

Differences of approach on INF were just one element in a growing divergence of security priorities between the US and their

71

European allies. Other examples included President Reagan's 1985 Strategic Defence Initiative. SDI was seen by pro-nuclear and pro-NATO European governments as an implicit dumping of the 'flexible response' strategy in favour of a scientifically imposs-ible defensive 'shield' to protect missile silos in the US against possible nuclear attack. Eventually, seeing that the President would not be deterred from pursuing SDI, most European NATO governments muted their reservations and pressed instead for a share of the lucrative science and technology contracts handed out by the Americans as part of their SDI programme.

Differences over specific weapons systems were only one source of discord within the NATO alliance. Since the advent of the Nixon Administration in the 1970s there have been tensions within the alliance on a variety of issues, including commercial interests and foreign policy towards 'out of area conflicts' in the Middle East, Africa and Latin America.

In the view of the European NATO member states, recent US Administrations have tended to pursue narrow American interests and to place less weight on the views and interests of their allies. The trend accelerated under the Carter Administration, with its unpredictable foreign policy gyrations, and a Reagan Adminis-tration which has sometimes been openly sceptical about the value and priority of America's European commitments.[14]

It was, to some extent, in anticipation of these stresses that the leading European NATO governments decided in 1982 to revive the Western European Union. The WEU had been launched in 1954, at the height of the Cold War, to coordinate the defence policies of Britain, France, Belgium, Holland, Italy, Luxembourg and West Germany. When the proposed European Defence Community failed to materialize, the WEU became dormant. Now it has been revived as a forum where Europeans can discuss defence policy without deference to the overweening presence of the United States, which dominates NATO itself.

The United States was far from happy at this development, despite the assurances of WEU states that all they intended was a stronger 'European pillar' for the NATO alliance. In 1983 the Reagan Administration warned its allies against deciding policy without the presence and participation of the United States. 'I do not think,' said Weinberger bluntly, 'it is a good thing to break into two blocs — one European and one American.'[15] In 1985 American diplomats attempted, with limited success, to restrict the range of policy issues discussed outside the NATO framework.[16] The Europeans again insisted that they had no intention of challenging US leadership or of building an alternative to NATO. But there was little doubt that they were making preparations for the gradual winding down of the 'American protectorate' in Western Europe. Indeed, subsequently, the WEU has been used by the British and French to spread the idea of greater European self-reliance in defence.

One striking manifestation of this new relationship has been the closer military cooperation between West Germany and France — which since de Gaulle's days has remained outside NATO's integrated military command — and especially an experiment in integrated Franco–German military units. While proceeding with extreme caution, Paris and Bonn have spoken of this as a 'prefigurative' attempt to create an integrated West European defence force which might involve other WEU countries at a later stage.

The French and West Germans have also discussed ways in which France's expanded nuclear 'Force de Frappe' — particularly its new medium-range nuclear missiles — might be extended to 'cover' West Germany. The implication remains — following the December 1987 INF agreement — that the French missiles may represent a substitute for the US Cruise and especially their Pershing 2 missiles.

Such neighbourliness on the part of the French government is not surprising: any future US withdrawal from Europe, together with Soviet overtures on West German economic cooperation, might otherwise result in a growing disengagement of the Federal Republic from NATO and a non-aligned West Germany.

On the other hand the French establishment is convinced that 'locking in' the Federal Republic's defence forces with those of its West European allies is not going to be enough. It has held intense discussions with the British government since 1986 on greater cooperation over nuclear policy. The French nuclear force is not readily compatible with Britain's American-supplied Polaris (to be replaced with an even more powerful American-supplied Trident system), and the USA discourages Britain from sharing data for as long as France remains outside NATO's integrated command.[17]

These questions were given an added urgency by the growing debate within the United States during the late 1980s over the withdrawal of all or part of the 326,000 troops committed to the defence of Europe. Some leading American strategists, such as the former Republican Secretary of State, Henry Kissinger, and the former Democratic National Security Adviser, Zbigniew Brzezinski, have made a case for transferring troops from Europe to areas such as the Middle East, and specifically the Persian Gulf.

US opinion has become increasingly sensitive to the ambiguous and divided responses of West Europeans to the American presence in Europe. American displeasure has mounted in the face of Europe's half-hearted support or even open opposition to American initiatives such as the US demand for economic sanctions against the Soviet Union and Libya and the bombing of Libya in 1986, ostensibly in reprisal for alleged Libyan support for terrorist organizations. In private US officials have become increasingly acerbic about the loyalty and reliability of their allies. One senior US official has been quoted as saying, 'The Europeans . . . hamper us on arms control. With the Soviet Union they pursue appeasement. In the Middle East they are working against us. Their interference is quite gratuitous.'[18]

As we have seen, the Americans have been deeply distrustful of European attempts to deepen economic and commercial links with the Soviet Union. And certainly during President Reagan's first term, which gave fullest expression to his hawkish anti-communism, the depiction of the Soviet Union as 'an evil empire' met with ill-disguised disapproval even from European NATO governments sympathetic to the United States and to President Reagan himself.[19]

There is also no doubt that even predominantly right-of-centre governments in Western Europe have been ready to defy US views and ignore US interests in key areas of foreign policy. In the Middle East, Europe has favoured alliance with the conservative Arab states over a closer relationship with Israel, which is

74

the priority of the United States. Even in America's own backyard of Central America, the EEC governments have refused to endorse US backing for the right-wing Contra guerrillas seeking to overthrow the Sandinista regime in Nicaragua.

These European 'betrayals' have been matched by the revised priorities of US policy makers in recent years, emphasizing the Pacific and other regions at the expense of European commitments. 'Should the US pull out of NATO?' asked an article in the *Wall Street Journal* in 1981 — and the conclusion drawn by the writer was surely a sign of the times. 'When we measure the near optimised markets of Europe and its 250 million persons against the near unoptimised 1.5 to 2 billion people of the Pacific basin, Europe seems a puny affair.' If few people would pose the choice so starkly, two distinct schools of thought do seem to have emerged within the United States in recent years. They might be dubbed 'Atlanticist' and 'post-Atlanticist'.

We can roughly identify the Atlanticist tradition with an older, liberal, east coast tradition — and also with areas of the country which have been in economic decline in recent decades. By contrast, post-Atlanticism is strongest in the economically stronger south and west where more right-wing and Pacific-oriented views hold sway.

It is no coincidence, for example, that the continued deployment of US Cruise and Pershing missiles in Europe never aroused much enthusiasm among the more right-wing post-Atlanticists in the Reagan Administration who were also the natural champions of the 'Star Wars' programme. They saw Europe-based missiles as constricting America's freedom of manoeuvre in securing a new strategic relationship with the Soviet Union, and their influence may have been a crucial element in Washington's readiness to sign an INF agreement with the Soviet Union when that became possible after the emergence of Secretary-General Gorbachev.[20]

Even Atlanticists have taken a tougher line on Europe of late. Politicians like Sam Nunn, the leader of the Democrats in the Senate, have hinted that they would support withdrawal of US troops unless European NATO governments agreed to shoulder a much bigger share of the costs of the defence of Europe (as much as $90 billion a year according to some estimates). 'The

American poor and working class are getting fed up with having to pay for the defence of the European rich and middle class,' was how Nunn put it.[21]

European objections to US policy and its leadership of the Western alliance fall into two conflicting camps. We have considered the response of the predominantly centre-right and Atlanticist governments of the European Community and NATO to the trend in US economic, foreign and security policy in recent years. But a significant proportion of Western European public opinion, and many left and centre-left political parties, remain suspicious of American government policy for very different reasons. Many Europeans are apprehensive about future US relations with the Soviet Union. Their alarm at the militantly anti-communist tenor of the first Reagan Administration has not been laid to rest by the the otherwise welcome signing of the INF agreement and the new interest in detente which became evident during 1986 and 1987.

These critics of US policy are not all in the same camp, of course. The leaders of the mainstream Western European social democratic parties, despite their reservations about US and NATO policy, nonetheless remain committed to membership of the Alliance and to preserving close links with the United States in the areas of security and foreign policy. More radical groups are committed to European disengagement from the Cold War military alliances. Having signed an agreement abolishing one class of nuclear weapon in Europe, the super-powers should, the European peace movement insists, proceed to abolish most, if not all, of those that remain. European critics of US policy are almost uniformly hostile to the concept of SDI and are sceptical about some of the US and NATO estimates of the scale of 'superiority' in conventional forces enjoyed by the Warsaw Pact over NATO.

Within the British Labour Party and the West German Social Democrats major strands of opinion challenge NATO's strategy in key respects. There is widespread opposition to the so-called 'first use' doctrine, under which the NATO alliance refuses to rule out the first use of nuclear weapons in a war, while insisting that it would never be the first to start hostilities.

Both parties are also unhappy about other aspects of NATO

76

war scenarios, including those which call for deep strikes behind enemy lines.[22] The Belgian and Dutch Labour parties have sought to reduce the 'nuclear tasks' allotted to their national armed forces under NATO's division of labour. Indeed the centre-right governments in both countries have already reduced these tasks, pleading in some cases that they cannot afford them.

The Danish and Norwegian governments, under social democratic pressure, still refuse to accept any US or NATO nuclear forces on their soil. The Danes are particularly unpopular with NATO strategists because of the influence of the social democrats, and more especially the openly neutralist People's Socialist Party which made big gains in the 1987 general election. They are blamed for the fact that Denmark has rarely met its NATO targets for defence spending in recent years.

The US and NATO cannot count on unqualified support in the Mediterranean countries, either. In Spain a mass movement against NATO membership narrowly lost a referendum on the issue in 1986. In order to defeat the anti-NATO movement the socialist government of Felipe Gonzales pledged itself to negotiate a reduction in US military bases. By the end of 1987 these negotiations were leading to strained relations between Washington and a government admired by the US and its major NATO allies for its austere and certainly non-socialist domestic policies.

Although the Italian and Portuguese governments are far more amenable to America's military requirements, there is opposition in both countries to new bases, relocated from Spain. In Greece there has been a long-standing confrontation between the US and PASOK, the left-of-centre government of Andreas Papandreou, over its demand for the closure of US bases.

Papandreou has cleverly avoided rupture with the United States over this issue, partly by using the bases as a pawn to limit US backing for Turkey, but there is no doubting the popularity of the call for the removal of the US military presence in the country. In Turkey the issue of foreign bases has not, as yet, been such a difficult one for NATO.

At least until it began to revise its policy following a third successive general election defeat in 1987, it was the British Labour Party's stance on security and defence that caused most anguish in the US and NATO establishments. Just before that election Caspar Weinberger, then US Secretary of State for Defence, left no doubt about Washington's view of Labour's commitment to the unilateral abandonment of Britain's own nuclear deterrent, support for the removal of US nuclear bases in Britain, and opposition to NATO's 'first use' strategy.

'Current Labour Party policies' would, he said, 'increase [US] isolationism and strengthen demands for the withdrawal of American forces from Western Europe.'[23] Speaking at about the same time, the then supreme commander of NATO forces in Europe, General Bernard Rogers, said Labour's policies of unilateral nuclear disaramament could lead to 'the break up of the NATO alliance'.[24]

The challenge on the European left to US and NATO policy is by no means limited to specific aspects of alliance strategy. Within the British Labour and other left parties some politicians are calling openly for withdrawal from NATO and positive 'non-alignment' towards the super-power military alliances.[25] This stand is taken even more forthrightly by what might be described as the New Left forces in Western Europe, the Green and independent left socialist parties.

France, of all the European countries, comes closest to a national consensus in favour not only of the Atlantic Alliance but of possessing its own nuclear forces. There is a certain irony in this because, since the period when de Gaulle dominated French politics, France has remained outside NATO's integrated military command.

That its 'outsider' status is changing is reflected in France's close cooperation on security policy with West Germany, including the creation of the pilot integrated Franco–German army brigade in 1987. This policy is enthusiastically endorsed by both the socialist President, François Mitterrand, and the Chirac government, led by the right wing.

Until very recently the consensus embraced even the traditionally pro-Soviet French Communist Party. The Party is now, apparently, reversing this policy, partly in reaction to French government plans to undertake a massive modernization and expansion of its nuclear missile forces. The Communist Party, however, now faces serious competition from a new political tendency made up of dissident communists and led by a former Communist Party leader, Pierre Junquin. The dissidents have the support of radical socialists, ecologists and sections of the far left, and are committed to a firmly anti-nuclear policy.

In Italy, too, there is substantial support for NATO and its nuclear strategy. On the left, the large and influential Italian Communist Party joins the small Italian socialist and social democratic parties in the nuclear camp. Indeed, the Italian Communist Party is more resolute in its support of NATO than some West European social democratic parties. The PCI leadership, in line with many European conservative and centrist parties, also supports the construction of a stronger 'European pillar' within the NATO alliance.[26]

Within the Party, however, there are now significant currents which take anti-nuclear and non-alignment policy positions in sympathy with the broad West European peace movement. And the gains made by a variety of small, anti-nuclear parties — notably the Greens, the Radicals and the Proletarian Democrats — were an interesting feature of the 1987 Italian general election.

The initial effect of the 1987 INF agreement was to reduce, marginally, the momentum of the radical peace movement in Western Europe. The British Labour Party's leaders appeared ready to abandon some of the party's unilateralist policies and to minimize its differences with both NATO and the US. But elsewhere in Western Europe there were, at the start of 1988, few signs that opposition to NATO orthodoxy was abating. This may reflect the growing, if limited, electoral impact of the Green and 'New Left' parties. The system of proportional representation, which operates in all West European countries except the United Kingdom, means that a Green or radical left party that scores between 10 and 20 per cent of the vote, as some have done in recent years, can exercise real influence nationally.

Equally important is a widespread mood of expectation: many people now believe that the ideological and political structures underpinning the Cold War are beginning to give way. The Gorbachev regime in the Soviet Union, with its policies of *glasnost* (openness) and *perestroika* (restructuring) has placed a new emphasis on arms reductions and steps to improve relations between East and West. There is little doubt that Soviet initiatives have encouraged the revival of debate about foreign policy alternatives on the European left.

The 'Soviet threat' to Western Europe is less credible, which is not to say that, even on the left, the Gorbachev reforms arouse high expectations. The radical European peace movement remains strongly critical of the totalitarian nature of Soviet and East European society, and the political, economic and social changes supported by the radicals go far beyond the reforms proposed by the Soviet leadership.

West Europeans are also aware that the pro-Moscow regimes in Eastern Europe are under immense strain. Indeed, at the start of 1988 there were suggestions that Poland, Hungary, Romania and Yugoslavia were heading for economic crises and serious social unrest. Increasingly West Europeans are asking just how reliable the peoples of Eastern Europe would be as Soviet allies in the event of hostilities. This undermines that fear of the omnipotence of the Soviet Union which was such a factor in shaping public attitudes during the early years of the Cold War in the 1940s and 1950s.

Coordinating organizations like European Nuclear Disarmament deliberately maintain close links with 'dissident' Eastern bloc peace groups as well as formally correct but distant relations with the Warsaw Pact governments. This policy has, in the past, provoked bitter denunciation of END and its affiliated organizations by official, government-sponsored peace groups in the Soviet Union and Eastern Europe.

In the aftermath of the INF agreement, many Europeans emphasize the need to accelerate the disarmament process. Pressure for agreements eliminating Europe-based battlefield nuclear weapons is especially strong in West Germany. There are also impatient calls for major reductions in conventional forces, and demands for the withdrawal of all foreign forces from European soil. Accelerated disarmament may depend on whether, over the next few years, the electoral pendulum swings in favour of parties of the left and centre-left in Western Europe. At the end of 1987 there were indications of a modest revival of the left — though not necessarily of the mainstream social democratic parties — in Belgium, Denmark, some of the West German regions, and Italy.

It is far from certain that current NATO nuclear strategy would survive the election of left-of-centre governments or coalitions in key European NATO countries. Such governments could quickly find themselves at odds with the policy of maintaining a strong nuclear element in the NATO arsenal. The return to office in Bonn of the West German social democrats, especially if they have to rely on the support of the Greens, might prove particularly awkward for NATO and the United States. Some Alliance strategists fear a terminal decline in the organization if Bonn's support begins to waver.

The stock market crash of October 1987 inevitably revived debate about the future scale of America's overseas military commitments. Although a succession of NATO ministerial meetings formally restated the United States' willingness to maintain those commitments, doubts persisted. In part these related to financial pressure within the US for major reductions in military spending. At the same time there was concern that transatlantic conflicts such as the episodic threats of trade war might spill over and sour defence relations. Conscious that the signing of the INF agreement might boost rather than weaken the influence of the anti-nuclear peace movement, the British and French governments made it clear that in their view denuclearization had gone far enough. Indeed, the British government went so far as to suggest that it might wish to make up the loss of medium-range, ground-launched US missiles by increasing the numbers of both air- and sea-launched missiles operating out of American bases in the UK.[27]

At the same time the European NATO governments launched a public relations exercise to convince voters that there could be no further negotiations on nuclear arms reduction until there had been a major, and asymmetrical reduction in conventional forces in Europe. This was justified by repeated references to the alleged 'overwhelming superiority' in conventional forces of the Warsaw Pact, a doctrine that has come under increasing challenge. Reports in 1986 by the London-based Institute for Strategic Studies, and by the defence committee of the Western European Union Parliamentary Committee in 1987 produced detailed critiques questioning this NATO assumption.[28]

According to these critics, while the Warsaw Pact undoubtedly had greater numbers of soldiers, the disparity was far less than the 3:1 advantage military doctrine asserts is the minimum needed by any aggressor to be confident of success. The difference in the findings partly turned on whether the forces of Spain (a new member state) and France (not in the integrated military command) should be counted on the Western side. The critics also pointed to the considerable gap in training and effectiveness between the conscript armies of the Warsaw Pact and the largely professional NATO forces.

The question of European security policy — in what may turn out to be the post-Atlanticist 1990s — is thus a highly divisive and controversial question among Europeans. And in the aftermath of the super-powers' INF agreement — and their attempts to negotiate 'deep cuts' in their respective arsenals of strategic nuclear weapons — the issue of what kind of defence and foreign policy is right for Europe seems to overshadow much else in the years immediately ahead.

Both NATO and the Western European Union face uncertain futures. The WEU is vulnerable to swings in the politics of its member states as regards both nuclear policy and the attempt to convince Europeans that they should shoulder a bigger share of the burden of NATO defences carried at present by the United States. As NATO strategists never tire of pointing out, nuclear weapons are a cheaper form of military power than conventional weapons in terms of 'the bang you get from your buck'.

But the anti-nuclear mood of most European societies seems likely to deepen rather than diminish. In a sense the limited nuclear arms reduction agreements signed by the United States and the USSR have 'legitimized' the European anti-nuclear movement. It is also unlikely that WEU governments will win the political argument for much bigger spending on conventional arms, especially if the collapse of the US dollar and the world stock markets in 1987 is followed by slower economic growth or a world economic recession.

Then there is the unresolved question of the relationship between NATO, the WEU and the EEC. The present seven-nation WEU does not want to weaken NATO further but is divided about whether gradually to merge the defence questions dealt with by the WEU with the security and arms control issues which are the domain of the EEC. This is something advocated strongly by Belgium and some non-EEC states.

Some of the EEC governments which hold heterodox views of NATO's nuclear strategy — such as Greece, Spain and Denmark, as well as neutral Ireland — might not support the assumption of greater responsibilities for defence. The US Administration is alarmed at the mere suggestion that the EEC might take over some of NATO's workload, partly because of the presence in the EEC of these awkward states; the Americans would be even more nervous if, over the next few years, neutrals such as Austria and Sweden were to join the Community.

On the other hand this is the direction in which the European Parliament wishes to go, supported strongly by leaders such as the President of the European Commission, Mr Jacques Delors.[29] And to the extent that arms policy has major economic, industrial and technological consequences, the European Community is almost bound to become involved in security strategy.

It is not possible to predict the shape of Europe's decision-making institution for defence and security. Much will depend on whether the United States, under the impact of changing geo-political considerations and the pressures of the financial crisis, begins to run down its commitment to NATO. Either way, questions of defence and foreign policy are going to loom larger on the European agenda than they have for the past thirty years.

We can conclude that the creeping regionalization of the world economy, and within that the growing strains within the Atlantic economic and security system, may face Europeans with some stark choices in the remaining years of this century. Decisions about economic strategy are bound to be influenced by the challenges of global crisis, of industrial restructuring, and increasing unemployment in Western Europe.

Will the EEC and Western Europe as a whole be content to allow the restructuring of their economies to be determined by free market forces? If economic crisis and unemployment persist, will demands not grow for alternative economic strategies based on new forms of European supra-national democratic planning and innovatory forms of public ownership at local, national and European levels?

Other questions arise concerning the kind of society in which Europeans want to live. Most pressing of all, Europeans will have to decide how best to assure their security. Will it lie in perpetuating the Cold War system — though without the economic and military backing of America? Will the peoples of Western Europe be willing to bear the sacrifices necessary to reconstruct the nuclear and conventional defences some believe will be necessary if the United States withdraws?

As an alternative, might it be possible for Europe to pursue new approaches to coexistence between East and West and, beyond that, to begin to build a wider European unity from the Atlantic to the Urals? Could political change in Western Europe and a radical transformation of society in Eastern Europe not combine to make this a practical proposition in the 1990s?

4
Agriculture: The Awkward Cornucopia

The most vivid image of the European Community in recent years has been a damning one: the contrast between world famine and Europe's surplus food mountains. That millions of people should endure hunger and malnutrition while EEC stockpiles groan with unwanted food is widely regarded as a human tragedy and a political obscenity.

For more than twenty years the defenders of the European Common Agricultural Policy were at least as numerous, and considerably more influential, than its critics. This is far from being the case today. The CAP as currently constructed is almost universally discredited in the eyes of EEC taxpayers and consumers, who have long criticized its excesses, and of growing numbers of farmers as well.

In 1987 farm spending accounted for some two-thirds of the entire European Community budget of more than £30 billion. The bulk of this went on guaranteed price support for farmers, the cost of storing surplus food, and the use of export subsidies to dispose of it on world markets.

Worse still, in its twilight years the CAP has become a byword for fraud on a grand scale. According to one estimate produced by the European Parliament,[1] fraud involving EEC agricultural subsidies and grants might well amount to some £2 billion a year. There have even been allegations that organized crime syndicates, including the Sicilian Mafia, have participated in EEC farm frauds, olive oil in southern Italy being a speciality. (These led to the Commission setting up a special anti-fraud squad to step up investigation into alleged abuses.)[2]

The basic flaw in the CAP is the system of guaranteed prices

85

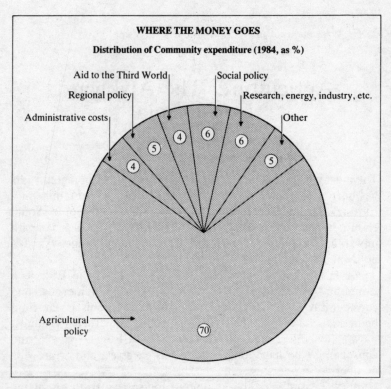

WHERE THE MONEY GOES

Distribution of Community expenditure (1984, as %)

The Common Agricultural Policy: a giant maw swallowing the EEC's resources. Agricultural commitments dwarf spending on social policy or research.

Source: Community revenue and expenditure account

for production without, until recently, any limit relating total output to market demand. The relatively high prices which have been set, notionally to help small peasant farmers, have encouraged overproduction by the heavily capitalized, high output farmers who have come to dominate EEC agriculture. There was nothing inevitable about this approach and, at least in theory, the architects of the CAP might have opted for a very different design. It might have been possible, for instance, to structure subsidies and financial support to guarantee farmers' incomes, instead of maximizing production without regard for social costs.

It must be admitted that the explosive growth of EEC farm production could not have been forecast with any accuracy by those who designed the CAP between the launching of the EEC in 1957 and the introduction of the policy in 1964. During those years a revolution in farming techniques occurred, including a massive extension of mechanization, the greater use of fertilizers, herbicides and pesticides, and genetic improvements of crops and animals which transformed agricultural productivity. The pace of change has redoubled in the past ten to fifteen years with the spread of 'industrial' farming systems.

One gets an idea of the scale of this growth in farm productivity when it is recalled that in 1957 more than 25 per cent of the population of the EEC countries worked on the land: thirty years later, the figure has fallen by almost two-thirds to less than nine per cent. Milk yields have risen by 50 per cent per cow in the same period and threaten to rise by another 40 per cent according to advocates of the use of new growth and production stimulators — notably Bovine Somatatrophine – 120, still untested.[3]

As we shall see later, this staggering boost to farm productivity has been achieved at a heavy price, not just in dearer food and food surpluses. Many of the new mass production techniques for poultry, fruit, vegetables — have resulted in a decline in the quality and palatability of food, signalled by a consumer backlash against excessive use of chemical fertilizers and support for organic farming.

Excessive cereal production is damaging the environment of whole regions, as hedgegrows are destroyed and small and medium-sized holdings are merged or bought out. Vast 'prairie' farms despoil the environment, threaten wild life, and destroy a visual and recreational amenity increasingly valued by people who live in high-density cities. In the new, industrialized agriculture there is little room for the social figure most people still readily identify with the rural landscape, the small farmer driven from the land with tragic consequences for rural communities in many regions of the EEC.[4]

This nightmare is not the dream of the founders of the European

Community, or of the architects of the CAP itself. They never envisaged that, thirty years on, the CAP would stand as the sole, rather desolate beacon of what the Community has achieved. They had seen it as just one important piece in a European jigsaw which would include common policies on industry, technology, economic strategy, social rights and many other issues. The grotesque imbalance in EEC budget expenditure is a measure of the excesses of the CAP, but its underlying cause must be sought in the EEC's failure to devise common social, industrial and other policies as a framework for the new Europe.

There is no longer any serious challenge to this analysis of where the CAP went wrong. It is shared, for instance, by the man who, more than any other single individual was the CAP's architect —the former Dutch Agriculture Commissioner, Sicco Mansholt. Interviewed for Granada Television's 'Trading Places' series, Mansholt explained that it had never been intended to create surpluses: 'Surpluses are the result of production and high productivity. You can see the same thing in the United States. The Common Market is responsible insofar as without it there would not have been any agricultural policy — then of course the market would be very low and the farmers would be very poor.'

Mansholt blames not the original policy but the political weakness of the Council of Ministers which proved unable to change the policy when surpluses, not potential shortages, became the dominant problem: 'When there is a danger of surpluses you have to take decisions to curb the process; to produce less. In the past twelve years decisions have not been taken in that direction. Only now has the Commission a policy, but the Council of Ministers are not taking the decisions.'

There is no doubt that the impact of a serious strategy to reverse the trend to overproduction will have harsh effects on the farming community. Mansholt's favoured solution is the 'set aside' approach, under which land is deliberately taken out of production and the farmer compensated. That, he believes, could help to tackle the cereals surpluses. But meanwhile, technological development continues inexorably:

'The difficulty is that in one generation's time — that is thirty-five

88

years — we will produce the same amount of foodstuffs on half of the cultivated area of today. So the cultivated area has to go down to fifty per cent of today. That is going to hurt farmers. Here in Holland during the past twenty years we have seen the proportion of our population engaged in farming fall from twelve per cent to six per cent and we can be sure that in a generation's time for farm population will be three per cent of all working people in Europe.'

It was recognized from the outset that without an agricultural policy the original agreement between the six founding member states, and notably between France and West Germany, would be seriously flawed. Even in those years it was clear that the Federal Republic would be the prime economic beneficiary of the creation of a common market, given its developing industrial power.

On the other hand, the customs union offered little to the tens of millions of EEC citizens who lived off the land, notably the mass of poor peasant farmers who dominated farming in France and Italy during the 1950s and 1960s. The CAP was designed not only to redress the urban-rural balance but also to bring the advantages offered to France and Italy closer to those enjoyed by the more industrialized countries of the EEC.

The principle of a common agricultural policy was therefore written into the Treaty of Rome, notably in Articles 38 to 47. These provided that a common market would apply to agriculture and trade in agricultural products (including fisheries). The objectives of the CAP were also set out: to increase agricultural productivity by promoting technical progress and the rational development of agricultural production; to ensure a 'fair standard of living' for the farming community; to 'stabilize markets' and to ensure that food reached consumers at 'reasonable prices'. Ironically, in view of later developments, the chapter of the Rome Treaty dealing with commercial policy states that the establishment of a customs union should 'contribute to the harmonious development of world trade', the progressive abolition of restrictions on international trade and the lowering of customs barriers.[5]

To achieve these goals the Treaty envisaged a common organization of agricultural markets, including rules on competition, compulsory coordination of the various national marketing organizations and their eventual replacement by a European body. This, when it was created, would regulate prices, production and marketing aids, and storage facilities; it would also set up a system for stabilizing imports into and exports from the Community.

The signatories of the Treaty of Rome acknowledged the need to reform the structure of farming in the Community to make it more competitive, but insisted this should occur 'without any threat to family farms'. It was explicitly recognized that the low level of world food prices would require EEC common prices to be higher — to 'provide adequate earnings' but 'without this being an incentive to over-production'. With hindsight the naïve optimism of these formulations is painfully clear.

It should, of course, be remembered that when the system was devised — it took seven years and involved a major constitutional row with France — no one thought of surpluses as a 'problem'. The abiding fear and preoccupation of agricultural policy makers was the shortage and insecurity of food supplies. In the late 1950s, millions of Europeans still had vivid memories of food shortages and semi-starvation in large parts of the European continent just a decade earlier.

By refusing to attend the Messina conference in 1955, which prepared the ground for the Treaty of Rome, Britain lost its opportunity to help shape the Community's future agricultural policy. The belated and ambivalent character of British interest in EEC membership, combined with a French-orchestrated campaign to keep the UK at bay, meant that British influence on the CAP was negligible.

When Britain did negotiate entry terms in 1973, it was in a weak position to demand a complete revision of policy. By then the CAP was set in concrete. British government negotiators were able to achieve reasonably generous transitional arrangements cushioning consumers, tax payers and the UK's traditional Commonwealth suppliers of cheap food from the full force of the CAP. By winning guarantees on access to the EEC market for New Zealand dairy exports, Britain indirectly contributed to the crisis of overproduction.

By the 1960s the predominant concern of EEC policy makers

was still the danger of future food shortages, even though post-war food rationing had long been abandoned. They were also aware that farm incomes were, in general, still far below the rapidly rising average incomes of the expanding industrial sectors of the European economy. Conditions in these years were grist to the mill of the EEC farming lobbies.

In the subsequent decade the CAP grew in both scope and complexity. Detailed marketing and price support regimes were negotiated for literally dozens of products. To counteract the disruptive effect of diverging national currency exchange rates on the unity of the agricultural market, a special system of 'green' exchange rates was devised. The idea was to prevent a situation where the devaluation of a currency led to higher farm prices — denominated in European Units of Account — in any one country.

In 1968, Sicco Mansholt, introduced an agricultural moderniz-ation strategy which deliberately encouraged larger and more productive farm units. But the task of preserving the common agricultural market in the face of disruptive upheavals on currency markets required the introduction of a system of frontier farm trade subsidies and levies of truly nightmarish complexity. Known as Monetary Compensatory Amounts (MCAs), the levies and subsidies, introduced in 1969, had to be adjusted weekly to prevent the agricultural market splintering and thus eventually undermining the whole CAP. Thus a country with a weak currency and an overvalued green exchange rate had its farm exports taxed, while one with a strong currency and an undervalued green exchange rate received what was in effect an export subsidy.[6]

This proliferation of bureaucratic and monetary controls soon became the subject of intense and frequently disruptive bargaining by the member states, particularly during the annual session held each spring to fix EEC farm prices. Worse than that, the system of agricultural exchange rates and compensatory MCAs sheltered national governments from having to come to terms with the full consequences of the rapid escalation in the overall annual cost of the CAP.

This was as true for successive British ministers of agriculture as for farm ministers from other countries with larger and more influential agricultural lobbies. Both Labour and Tory farm ministers, during the 1970s and 1980s, were frequently in the enviable position of being able to sound off against extravagant overall farm price increases while eventually securing adjustments to the British green exchange rates which brought higher sterling prices to UK farmers. Given the super-profits made from the CAP, particularly by the biggest and wealthiest British farmers, it is not surprising that they gradually became evangelists of the CAP's virtues.

One of the startling features of the annual farm price negotiations in the EEC during these years was the remarkable political autonomy enjoyed by farm ministers even within their own national governments. It became obvious that while finance ministers could denounce the extravagance of the CAP, this did not necessarily bind their cabinet colleagues, the farm ministers. Nowhere had this ministerial autonomy been displayed more blatantly than in the Federal German Republic — the country responsible, more than any other, for pushing up the underlying costs of the CAP.

In popular EEC mythology France, not Germany, has played the role of CAP villain. Successive British governments as well as the British media have blamed France's 'inefficient peasant farmers' for propping up the high-cost CAP, and commended West German governments for their insistence on EEC budget rectitude. This is wrong on several counts. As we shall see, the primary beneficiaries of the EEC agricultural policy have been not the small but the largest farmers — including the agro-business corporations which have been responsible for mass production and prairie-style farming in much of northern Europe in recent years.

Indeed there has been a perceptible widening of the income and prosperity gap between large and small farmers throughout the European Community in the past two decades. Certainly twenty-five years of the CAP have not achieved a transformation in the lot of small farmers. Yet their protection has been the main ideological justification offered by EEC governments for the spiralling cost of a farm policy based on high prices.

On two main counts the West German government must bear specific responsibility for the maintenance of an irresponsible

Community farm policy, when all the indicators pointed to the need for reform. First, West Germany has led demands for high, guaranteed cereal prices, even though higher grain prices immediately elevate other agricultural costs, notably the price of animal feedstuffs.

Second, the West German government has encouraged a significant sector of part-time or 'weekend' farms. These are holdings maintained by people who draw their primary incomes from industry or other non-agricultural occupations. This farm lobby is particularly strong in some of the south German regions, such as Hesse and Bavaria, dominated by the conservative Christian Democratic and Christian Social Union parties.

There is nothing reprehensible in such a policy, which can be defended on environmental and social grounds. What is at issue is that the European Community's highly restricted budget, rather than the far greater resources of the Federal German and regional German budgets, should be used to finance these farmers. Worst of all, successive West German governments have insisted on employing high price guarantees, rather than direct income aids, as the primary means of subsidizing part-time farming.

In West Germany as a whole the average farm size is small — around 16 hectares — compared with an average of 28 in France. According to official statistics, which some experts hold to be unreliable on this question, at least 45 per cent of farmers are part-time.

West Germany, like Britain, is a net importer of food, and might be thought to have a vested interest in curbing excesses and high-cost production. Moreover the Federal Republic is by far the largest single net contributor to the Community budget — in a real sense, the European Community's 'paymaster'. It thus appears to have an overriding 'national' interest in securing agricultural reform.

But there is more to the German paradox than that. The rural community enjoys a semi-mythological status in the philosophy of West German conservatism. There are genuine social reasons for maintaining small farming units and viable rural communities, and this is a goal which the left-wing West German Green party shares with the traditionalist right. Yet there is rarely any serious debate in West Germany about the wider economics of support for farming. The Greens and the social democratic Left, unlike the CDU/CSU, do not believe that only indiscriminate price guarantees can make such communities viable. They would prefer income support and other incentives, whether paid for by Brussels or Bonn, to aid part-time farming.

The truth is that a relatively small number of farming votes play an inordinately important role in West German politics. The rural vote has long been seen as a key social constituency by the Christian Democrats and above all by their Bavarian allies, the Christian Social Union.[7] Time and again when the issue of agricultural reform has forced its way on to the agenda at EEC ministerial meetings, the Christian Democrats have played the 'farming card'. The result has been consistent failure to grapple with some of the least defensible aspects of the CAP, above all high grain prices. And so West Germany continues to use EEC farm price increases as a mechanism for transferring economic resources, paid for mainly by itself, to its own farmers.

Outside West Germany, the primary beneficiaries of the CAP have been the largest and most 'industrialized' agricultural interests. As their productivity intensifies — rewarded by guaranteed high prices — so, inexorably, the well-known food mountains and lakes extend. In the closing months of 1987, these surpluses were still enormous — both literally and as a source of political embarrassment. Milk powder stocks totalled 746 tonnes, grain stocks 13.1 million tonnes, butter stocks one million tonnes and beef stocks 715,000 tonnes. In 1987 the cost of financing these and other intervention stocks came to about seven billion pounds, quite apart from the cost of disposing of them through export subsidies, two-thirds of which is borne by the EEC budget and one-third by the budgets of national EEC governments.[8]

According to British government figures, in 1987 EEC wheat prices were 51 per cent higher than the world average, butter prices about 80 per cent higher, and the beef price differential highest of all at a staggering 90 per cent.

It is important to realize that the CAP is a highly complex system and the mode of intervention differs for different categories of product. The CAP operates through a series of market organizations designed to maintain high prices for farmers. They vary from one sector to another, depending on the nature of the farm product and the outcome of complex internal negotiations between the member states within the Community.[9]

First, there are measures to support internal prices, which cover 72 per cent of all farm production. These range from buying in of surplus production at the intervention price (for example grain, beef and dairy products such as butter and milk powder), through private storage subsidies (pig meat) to withdrawal of surplus production from the market for wine and for distribution to those on social security (food handouts by charitable organizations for the most part) or recycling as animal feedstuffs (fruit, vegetables and milk powder).

Second, there are direct income subsidies. These take the form of deficiency payments for oilseeds, protein crops and fibre plants — most of which are only partly protected against import competition, making it impossible to maintain prices. In addition, farmers in some of the poorer regions of the EEC receive special income supplements. This is the path which many CAP reformers want to take in the future.

Third, there are measures to control imports: these affect all agricultural output except oilseeds. Controls are imposed whether the Community is self-sufficient in a particular product or not.

Products subject to intervention imported from outside the Community are liable to variable import levies. These are designed to ensure that they cannot come in below a given price level, normally 10 per cent above the prevailing internal intervention price. When the Community itself is in surplus these levies effectively keep out all competitor products, except those exempted by special agreements.

In the case of wine, fruit and vegetables, the EEC relies on import tariffs, combined with minimum prices, but these are less effective than the system of variable import levies. For certain commodities such as soya and other oil seeds, including fodder seeds, no import controls are imposed because of GATT free trade rules. But in 1987 the Commission pressed hard for a tax on all vegetable oils and fats. Although this was intended in part to restrict domestic EEC output it was also aimed at foreign

95

producers. Predictably, it was denounced in the United States and Third World countries as another example of EEC agricultural protectionism.

The European Community sugar regime, designed to aid European beet sugar growers, has always been resented by poorer countries producing cheaper cane sugar in the Caribbean and elsewhere. Under the regime there are three quotas: the 'A' quota is fixed at a level equal to current internal consumption; the 'B' quota is a small extra production allowance to cover potential shortfalls and like the 'A' quota it benefits from guaranteed price support; finally, there is a 'C' quota which receives no guaranteed price and which has to be sold on the world market without subsidies.

The scheme is partly financed by levies on producers and, more especially, on sugar refiners and processers. The net result is that EEC sugar beet farmers are paid, on average, five times the going world rate for their sugar. The African, Caribbean and Pacific former European colonies, associated with the EEC through the Lome Convention, are given special concessions on their sugar exports, but Third World countries as a whole are hit hard by the policy.

The world-wide growth of sugar production for export has depressed the world price far below production costs even in the poorest Third World countries. The EEC's dumping of surplus 'C' and 'B' quota sugar — more than 30 per cent of total world exports — is the major cause of the permanent price depression. It would help if EEC price supports and subsidies — at a lower level — were restricted to 'A' quota production, covering the internal needs of the EEC. At present the excess support of the 'A' and 'C' quotas allows the highly efficient EEC producers to subsidize export of the 'supported' 'C' quota sugar. One solution might be to require the EEC sugar regime to raise the full amount of its subsidies by increasing substantially the present levies on growers and processers.

Finally, the CAP maintains high prices through its measures to encourage exports. These involve the notorious export 'restitutions' or refunds, which are designed to bridge the gap between internal EEC prices and the usually much lower world prices.

Refunds are also paid on non-intervention products such as fruit and wine destined for specific export markets. This system is the heart of the Community's system for disposing of its high-cost internal surpluses on lower-cost world markets without under-mining prices paid to European farmers. It is, of course, the single most provocative feature of the CAP in the eyes of the rest of the world.

The extent to which the CAP is directly, let alone solely respon-sible for the appalling problems facing farmers in the Third World is a hotly disputed question in the EEC and internationally. The United States, which waxes indignant over the iniquities of the CAP, itself bears its share of responsibility for global overpro-duction. This continues today despite — or perhaps because of — the crisis which has hit American farming since the mid-1980s.

There are 2.3 million farming units in the US, 1.6 million of which are small farms whose proprietors or tenants eke out a barely adequate living. No less than 60 per cent of all American farmers receive income from outside interests or employment and, while there are only a fifth as many farmers as there were in the 1930s, annual increases in productivity — around 12 per cent in recent years — continue to outstrip those in other major agricul-tural countries.

Contrary to popular impressions and the propaganda of some Washington politicians, the US taxpayer pays about $26 billion a year in one way or another to compensate US farmers for low prices and the slump in their incomes. On average each US farm is subsidized to the tune of about $30,000 — five times the level of state aid under President Carter in the 1970s.

American farmers growing wheat, maize and rice in 1987 benefited from US prices which were between 40 per cent and 150 per cent higher than prevailing world prices. Yet US government officials point out, with some justice, that for the most part federal support for farmers has not involved underpinning artificially high prices. Instead it has taken the form of income maintenance and compensation to farmers who 'set aside', or leave idle, land which might otherwise add to the production surplus.

The net effect of the US system is nonetheless that a greater volume of farm output finds its way on to depressed world markets than would be the case if support was curbed. The US has challenged the EEC to negotiate away all forms of subsidies by the end of the century, but this is a propaganda bluff. The influence of the US farming lobby during both Congressional and Presidential elections is such that American commitment to the abolition of farm subsidies is unlikely to be tested on the hustings.

Although other food exporters are not without sin there is no doubt that the EEC and the US are mainly responsible for market conditions which undermine the viability of Third World peasant farming. The flight from the land in so many African, Latin American and Asian countries is generating an appalling urban crisis of poverty, homelessness and chronic unemployment. In such a context the efforts of the EEC (through the Lome Convention) to provide aid to Third World commodity producers appear worthy but somewhat marginal.

The World Bank has attempted to calculate who would win and who would lose if an unrestricted free trade system was implemented for agriculture on a global basis.[10] This purports to show that Third World countries would be about $18 billion a year better off, the industrial world $46 billion better off, and the 'Communist' Eastern bloc countries $18 billion worse off.

These figures disguise a number of conflicting trends within each global grouping. In the so-called Third World consumers would be massively worse off, while the farmers of the advanced industrialized countries would be no less than $104 billion worse off. It is nevertheless true that in the Eastern bloc both farmers and consumers would be especially vulnerable to global free trade in farm products.

The crisis in the Eastern bloc farm system has provided an enormous source of relief for the EEC since, thanks to perennial production shortfalls, the Soviet Union and Eastern Europe have been major importers of EEC dairy surpluses and US grain surpluses. Thanks to the operation of the Common Market system of export rebates, frequently it has been far cheaper for shoppers to buy EEC food in Leningrad or Moscow than in Luxembourg or Manchester. Needless to say, this is a situation which has further discredited the CAP in the eyes of the consumer within the European Community.

Of course, the governing elites in the Third World also bear a share of the responsibility for the crisis in indigenous Third World agriculture: to pay for expensive imported military equipment and other extravagances of the modern state, they have pressured peasant producers to produce crops for export rather than food for local consumption. Contraction of indigenous farming has increased the vulnerability of their peoples to the consequences of episodic natural disasters such as drought and famine.

The contrast between unwanted food surpluses and famine and hunger in the Third World has, naturally, led to the question, 'why not simply move the EEC food mountains to the Third World?' But recent studies[11] show that this is not as simple as it looks.

To start with, food gifts on any scale — while obviously justified by situations of famine, as in Ethiopia in the 1980s — actually depress the commercial viability of local farming. A country which has been given massive free food aid maybe less able to feed itself afterwards than it was before.

Moving food stocks costs the EEC more than normal export subsidies or storage payments, as the Ethopian famine relief operation showed. It is cheaper, if most offensive, to destroy food stocks outright. Indeed, over the years the EEC and national agricultural authorities have tolerated wholesale destruction of crops, despite the outcry. Feeding surplus dairy products back to cattle as feedstuffs is barely less objectionable. Other alternatives include attempts to convert surplus butter into industrial oils, surplus wine into industrial alcohol, and the proposal to convert surplus grain into biothenol as an energy source: all these schemes cost a great deal of money for little return.

Encouraging consumption of some European foods in the Third World also raises serious public health and dietary issues. During the 1970s it was discovered that African children fed with EEC milk powder reacted very badly; there have also been adverse results when people have been encouraged to switch to grains which are not traditional in their local diet.

Making food available to those who need it can be a costly item in EEC or national government budgets. Resources have to be made available to those distributing free food if it is to reach the hungry. Indications are that, in future, the EEC authorities will proceed more cautiously with such schemes, emphasizing better preparation and supporting finance.

The Commission can say, with justice, that reform of the CAP is under way. New disciplines — including lower price increases to farmers, production quotas for milk and other products, reductions in the guaranteed thresholds of price support, and 'co-responsibility' levies imposed on producers — are beginning to have an effect. In September 1987 the Commission estimated that national 'savings' as a result of these measures had risen from £750 million to £4.2 billion in 1987 and an estimated £6 billion in 1988.

From the mid-1980s, under the impact of the growing budgetary crisis, EEC governments have with few exceptions come to accept the need to restrain overproduction. Milk and beef were the first targets of new curbs linking the level of price support to the scale of potential overproduction, a form of discipline which the agricultural Ministers may seek to apply more widely.

It is not yet possible to judge how effective the quotas will prove in eliminating the chronic dairy sector surpluses. That farmers in the key dairy producing countries were able to live with the quotas, and even sell them in a 'willing buyer' market, might suggest that they were still not harsh enough to guarantee an end to the milk 'lake'.

The price at which these quotas are currently changing hands — an average of £6000 for a quota based on the output of a single cow — is seen by many analysts as an indicator of the degree of 'excess profit' being earned by the efficient EEC milk producer. It should not be forgotten, either, that the current quota includes 11 million tonnes of milk surplus to domestic consumption. This means a continuing disposal cost in excess of 5 billion ecu per year.

On the eve of the December 1987 European Council — the periodic summit meeting of EEC heads of state and government — a major effort had been mounted to extend the principle of tight production regimes to the other key surplus agricultural products. Unfortunately, even as EEC farm ministers were grappling with this problem, the renewed slide in the international value of the dollar was pushing up the cost of export rebates. The governments of the twelve may well have concluded that theirs was the task of Sisyphus.

The solution to the 'German problem' which lies at the heart of CAP reform — and which is mainly, though not exclusively, about grain — hung on a resolution of the internal conflicts within the Bonn government. The issue facing the West German establishment was to decide whether the German farm interest was greater than that of the German taxpayer or the German consumer.

The problem of the Mediterranean products within the framework of CAP reform is potentially far more intractable. The southern Europeans indignantly point out that they have long paid for the follies of north European farmers and that the CAP has done little for them. Moreover north European industry has primarily benefited from the opening up of their home markets to EEC competition.

Feelings are becoming bitter in the newer Mediterranean member states — Greece, Portugal and Spain. All three countries agreed to far-reaching concessions in removing domestic protection against the industrial exports of other EEC countries. They now want some of the benefits of the CAP for their farmers. More important, they insist on a qualitative increase in the direct developmental flow of resources from the richer to the poorer member states through the regional and social funds.

This is what makes a Commission proposal to tax oils and fats so sensitive. In the Commission's eyes it would be *quid pro quo* for tougher controls on production of excess olive oil, raising revenues which would help to finance concessions to the southern Europeans. But the tax is highly unpopular with producers elsewhere — notably in the US and the Far East. The threat of an international agricultural trade war — not only with the US but with many Third World exporters of vegetable oils — would test to the full the EEC's commitment to avoiding such conflict.

The story of the proposed oils and fats tax is a typically arcane EEC affair. Because of the over-abundance of cereals, farmers were deliberately encouraged, by the use of subsidies, to switch to growing sunflower and rape seed. The trouble is that with the

101

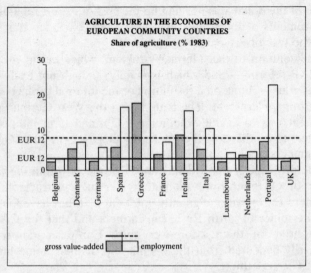

AGRICULTURE IN THE ECONOMIES OF EUROPEAN COMMUNITY COUNTRIES

Share of agriculture (% 1983)

gross value-added · employment

The poorer countries still rely heavily on agriculture for employment and prosperity.

Source: European Commission

resources of the EEC budget stretched to breaking point, the Commission feels that the only way it can pay for these subsidies is to introduce a tax on *all* vegetable oils and fats.

As Guy Walker, the President of the European Margarine Manufacturers Federation, told Granada, this would result in margarine prices going up by about 80 per cent.

Thus two political threats loom over the CAP reformers. The first is that reform could become, or be seen as, a 'north-south' issue if the southern Europeans decide that it is another means of denying them the advantages which their northern colleagues have long enjoyed.

Should a southern European political backlash develop in reaction to the attempted reform of the CAP it might spill over into the negotiations on the completion of the European Community's internal market. The long, complex and sometimes highly controversial business of removing all barriers to trade and the movement of capital will require southern European cooperation, without which 1992 may become a Utopian deadline.

There are also signs of a revolt by farmers in northern Europe. Reading the entrails of the general election in Denmark in September 1987 and subsequent regional elections in West Germany, it seems that a significant number of farmers may have withheld support from conservative and centre-right parties.

It is too soon to say whether a protest vote will become a mass defection, or whether this could be the factor that topples a succession of conservative governments in western Europe over the next few years. Even the most militant farmers' organizations and lobbies probably recognize the inevitability of CAP reform, which would suggest that the powerful CAP farm lobby is a diminishing threat to agricultural reformers.

That may change if and when significant numbers of farmers are forced to quit the land as a result of the measures already taken or likely to be taken to reduce and finally eliminate chronic food surpluses in the early 1990s. At that time the political will of governments ostensibly committed to reform will be put to the full test.

Reform is bound to have consequences outside as well as within the European Community. Agricultural products have provided the major flashpoint in trade conflicts between the EEC and the United States. Unresolved, the conflicts may multiply and the early 1990s may yet bring a transatlantic trade war.[12]

Precisely to avert this, there is pressure on the EEC to make agricultural trade one of the priorities for the Uruguay round of talks on international trade liberalization to be attended by the member governments of the General Agreement on Tariffs and Trade. There are still major differences of approach between the EEC and its GATT partners on the questions of what farm trade liberalization will involve and how quickly it will move ahead.

The more tangible the benefits of current CAP reforms become, in terms of lower surpluses and gradually reducing stocks of unwanted food, the easier it will be to agree on a common approach to long-term reform within GATT. But the issues involved in world farm trade go beyond the precise form of production or income support adopted by the EEC, the US or any other major world agricultural producer.

For example, it is going to be virtually impossible to plan the total phasing out of subsidies paid on exports of surplus farm produce from the Common Market while the currency used in international agricultural trade is the US dollar — given the disruptive decline in the dollar's international value in recent years.

It may be that the crisis of the US dollar in the late 1980s will prove to be the beginning of the end of its role as the world's trading and reserve currency. But the prospects of a global monetary agreement establishing a stable artificial currency unit are no brighter. A first step might involve reorganization around a grid of major global currencies, of which the European Currency Unit (ecu) would be one. But that would require an international agreement fixing the relative values of, say, the dollar, the ecu and the yen. And that would be an even more daunting task than the effort to strengthen the European Monetary System and the ecu within the European Community. It will raise exactly the same issues of economic and monetary convergence, but at a higher level: between the major world economies rather than between the economies of the EEC.

The reform of the CAP is, for all these reasons, going to be a long and hard road — all the more so if current efforts to tackle overproduction in the EEC lead to a significant flight from the land and unemployed farmers add to the queues of unemployed in the cities. Conversely economic recovery in Western Europe, if it reduced urban unemployment to manageable proportions and provided new jobs for those who leave the land, would make reform somewhat more feasible.

Wider issues than price and production levels are at stake in any long-term reform of the Community's agricultural policies. A food and environment policy is needed every bit as much as a farm policy in the narrow sense of the current definitions.

A food policy would embrace questions of quality and their relationship to diet and health. The bias of the Community's policies should encourage organic farming and reduced dependence on fertilizers and industrial farming systems.[13] Already special incentives are being introduced to assist diversification by farmers who abandon production of commodities in surplus. There is a practical limit, however, to the numbers of farmers who can be expected to expand into forestry, tourism, or other rural pursuits.

It is also going to take time to restore the lost balance in our environment brought about by the despoliation of commercial agriculture in recent decades. On the other hand the employment potential in the restoration and protection of the environment is likely to be far greater than conventional economic strategies have acknowledged.

Finally, a food aid policy which complements and does not undermine the development of Third World countries is going to take years to emerge. It will raise very fundamental questions about the nature of trade and aid relations between the industrialized countries and the poor, developing world as a whole.

The reform of the EEC Common Agricultural Policy, therefore, calls into question many aspects of the Western economic system. It remains to be seen whether the European Community has the political imagination to meet the challenge.

5
Bringing Down the Barriers

The world has shrunk, and Europe with it. In the age of Concorde distances in Europe pale into insignificance, and it isn't just the high flyers for whom travel is now commonplace. Better cars, faster motorways, more efficient railways now mean that journeys which even a generation ago were a once-in-a-lifetime affair for ordinary people can be fitted into a weekend round trip.

The affluent society, too, has played its part in bringing the benefits of travel within reach of the majority. Few Europeans have never been abroad. According to figures gathered in 1987, three-quarters of the British population have visited another EEC country at least once. The figures for France and Germany are much higher.[1]

Even the English Channel, for so long a formidable obstacle, is becoming little more than an inconvenience. The Channel Tunnel, with its high speed rail links between the major European capitals, is bound to weaken the traditional British sense of isolation from Europe still further.

It isn't just the annual holiday, either. Since cheap charter flights brought Spanish sun within easy reach of the ordinary holidaymaker in the Sixties, destinations have multiplied. Ski trips to the Alps in winter, weekend getaways and cross-Channel day trips mean that the rest of Europe is becoming less foreign for more and more people. School trips are granting a new generation of children the chance to travel abroad and meet other Europeans of their own age.

If this is true for the average Briton, it is even truer for those who live on the continent, where borders are even less of an obstacle; especially for the smaller countries like Holland and

Belgium where two hours on a motorway is normally more than enough to get you to the border.

Inevitably all this has affected how Europeans feel about each other. Even if differences remain (and no one would wish them away) Europeans of different nationality are no longer strangers. Even if they don't understand each other's languages as well as they might, they communicate. Each sees how the other lives. Their habits, national dishes and ways of life are no longer a mystery.

A glance at any supermarket shelf will confirm that eating habits travel well. The British have brought brie and camembert back from their French holidays as the colonial officials once brought back Indian curry. And just as the British ritual of tea drinking is giving way to coffee, the 'English breakfast' of bacon and eggs is much sought after by continentals. It would not be an exaggeration to say that much of the pressure for reform of the British licensing laws, among the most restrictive in Europe, has its source in the experience of Britons abroad, where cafes stay open day and night without any obvious increase in alcohol abuse.

If being European means anything — and in a recent poll nearly half those interviewed claimed a European as well as a national identity — it is largely because of the growing ease of travel, which according to the same poll was the second most striking development since the European Community was founded in 1958 (the first was the development of 'cooperation' and 'trust' between countries who have been at each other's throats for centuries). Significantly, many people would like to see travel made easier still: although border formalities are gradually relaxing, they are not being removed fast enough. The psychological barriers are coming down, but customs posts, officialdom and red tape remain as stubborn reminders that Europe is still a physically divided continent. Clearly, barriers which have grown up over the years aren't going to disappear overnight. But the arguments in favour of their removal are now gaining increasing acceptance, among European political parties and trade unions as well as industrialists.

The European Commission believes they can be dismantled. The Cockfield plan, as it is sometimes called, or 'The White Paper on Completing the Internal Market', to give it its full title, is now accepted EEC policy. Its author, Conservative peer Lord Cockfield, has set out a programme of 320 steps. Broadly, Community member states should agree that what is good enough for everyone else is good enough for them. Once minimum standards are reached, differences in the detail should not be accepted as the excuse for maintaining these barriers any longer. If that principle is accepted, and member states can be persuaded to narrow or remove altogether those differences in indirect taxation and excise duties which are the other major generator of paperwork, then truly the barriers could come down and Europe would be on the move.[2]

National flags are disappearing from customs posts to be replaced by the European flag with the name of the country in the ring of twelve golden stars which symbolize European unity. But as long as those posts are there at all, such gestures merely underline how far there is still to go. As far as border police and customs officials are concerned, the traveller is still a foreigner. A good many restrictions on what you can do remain and the men in peaked caps are there to see that those restrictions are enforced. They hold absolute sway over any traveller. They can arrest or detain, seize goods, search your person and your property. These are the first people most visitors come across when arriving in a country for the first time. It helps reinforce the image that other Europeans are all potential criminals.

Although duty-paid allowances now allow people to take as much as they can physically carry, the fact that there are limits at all keeps customs officers at work. Fill your boot with French wine or German beer and you are breaking the law, though your purchase was strictly legal. All taxes and duties have been paid. Your only crime is wanting to take your purchase home with you.

Customs officers are trained to sniff out smugglers, not to be their country's ambassadors. Instances of impolite or overzealous customs officials are still very common. A Belgian MEP, Willy Kuijpers, complained to the European Commission after constituents travelling in Italy had upset local customs officials quite unintentionally. They were in the Tyrol, a German-speaking part of Italy. To be polite, or so they thought, they began speaking in

108

German; unfortunately, this turned out to be the wrong thing to do. They found themselves subjected to checks stricter than those inmposed on French and other visitors.

A Dutch MEP, Teun Tolman, tells of a top European official who was driving to Holland from France to attend a conference on the common market. He arrived an hour late because of hold-ups at the border. Hardened European travellers will tell you it happens all the time. Andrew Pearce, MEP for West Cheshire and the Wirral, has been campaigning for years against rude customs officers, particularly at the busy ferry port of Dover. Most travellers put up with this treatment because they have no choice. Customs officers are armed with an array of powers often more formidable than those of the police. Arguing can get you into jail, and certainly won't get you through customs any faster.

Most Europeans believe that existing EEC legislation grants them the right to unhindered travel throughout the Community. That isn't the case. As the Commission told Dieter Rogalla, a German MEP who helped found the Kangaroo group of campaigners against frontiers, the right of free movement only applies to persons who are self-employed, providers or recipients of services or workers. The two main hindrances to abolishing passport checks are differences in social security entitlements arising out of different social security systems and the absence of a common visa policy for non-EEC nationals.

Moreover, in order to take advantage of that right you have to prove you are entitled to exercise it by showing a passport or identity card. When it comes to border police and customs officers you are once again automatically under suspicion until you can prove you are innocent. The unspoken thought behind the rules they are there to police is that unless you've come to make money or spend it, or otherwise make yourself useful, you've no rights whatsoever.

Even if you can get through, this is not necessarily true of your baggage. Customs officers are empowered to search travellers for a whole range of prohibited articles including live animals, drugs and pornography. Those countries which still operate exchange controls naturally extend customs checks to money too. Few would dispute the need to control movements of illegal drugs.

Every year customs and excise officers intercept millions of pounds worth of dangerous drugs as they cross the borders, though most drug cargoes are transported either by light plane or via secluded country roads.

The importing of pornographic material raises sensitive issues. Items have been confiscated at the border which are freely available in any shop, as was demonstrated recently when a British company took her majesty's customs and excise to the EEC Court of Justice in Luxembourg in protest at the confiscation of a consignment of inflatable sex dolls. Such prudery seems a poor justification for the inconvenience border controls cause to the majority of innocent travellers trying to go about their lawful business.

As for live animals, this particular restriction gives rise to its own crop of hard luck stories. Britain has by far the toughest rules about importing live animals. Most are subject to long periods of quarantine. Because it is an island the objective of keeping out dangerous diseases is at least feasible. The UK is still rabies free. But it keeps the courts busy with some amusing cases. Italian student Rosario Tropea was fined £300 by Uxbridge magistrates in West London after being caught smuggling by alert customs officers at London's Heathrow airport. He had concealed a 21-inch sand boa in his underpants. Another case involved a French student who was fined for bringing in his pet rat. Little is heard of the scores of people whose more conventional pets are confiscated every year. The government stoutly defends its right to maintain such controls in order to safeguard the health of the public.

Some rules can be defended. But these represent only a fraction of the total body of rules and regulations which justify the persistence of customs posts. Common sense would dictate that anything dangerous or illegal, whether poisonous, explosive, diseased or offensive — such as guns, bombs, drugs or stolen goods — should be contraband. Most people would be surprised, however, to learn that there is hardly any item save the clothes you stand up in which is not subject to some import restriction or other. Common sense has little to do with it.

One student who took his record collection with him on a study visit to France was stopped at Calais. The customs officer announced that he was entitled to take only thirty records with him, then waved him on. The student thought he was joking, but later a friend showed him a guide for foreign nationals wishing to take up residence in France. There it was, in black and white: his battered, scratched and otherwise worthless collection of punk classics could have been confiscated.

Much less fortunate was the Briton who fell foul of customs en route to an international conference of engineers in the sleepy spa town of Vittel. In his boot were 100 T shirts intended as free gifts for his colleagues. First he was stopped at Calais, where French customs officers pointed out that it was illegal to bring them in without the proper papers. When in exasperation he told them that in that case he would simply chuck them away, they promptly confiscated his passport and sent him back on the next Dover-bound hovercraft with orders not to return until he'd filled out the necessary forms. Of course, the inevitable happened: when he disembarked at Dover, British customs demanded he pay import duty on the T shirts. After hearing his explanation, the customs officer took pity on him and sent him off to get the required forms — which, by the way, could only be filled in by a shipping agent. Having crossed that hurdle — shipping agents are fortunately quite thick on the ground at Dover — he presented himself at customs £18 poorer, but at least with the necessary paperwork.

What he hadn't realised was this: carrying a boxful of T shirts doesn't only require expensive and time-consuming paperwork; it also turns a private passenger into freight. After standing with his box of T shirts in a queue of juggernauts, he was told he'd have to change his ticket. His freight had not been included on the ship's manifest. Carrying undeclared freight counts as fraud, he was told. Changing his ticket cost another £26. It also meant that he'd missed the 6 o'clock hovercraft he was due to take.

Officials now told him that his papers would have to be changed again as they were made out for the six o'clock crossing. Not surprisingly, he blew his top. Officialdom showed it can sometimes be human. They let him through. He arrived at Calais for the second item, seven hours later. This time his papers were in order and he was let through. One snag, though. The following day he

111

had to show up at the nearest customs point to his destination, Vittel–Epinal. Only he couldn't show up in person — another shipping agent had to be engaged. The final bill for a boxful of 100 T shirts worth £300 was a staggering £526. Judy Walker, the public relations officer for a London-based company who tells this story, adds as a footnote: 'Apart from the very first customs search not once did anyone look inside the box.'[3]

Such stories surface with amazing regularity. David Long, an Ulster artist, was forced to pay Irish customs £700 when officials at the border post of Tyholland spotted a portrait of boxing champion Barry McGuigan on the back seat of his car. Long was only taking a short cut through the Republic on the way from his home in Bangor to an official presentation of the painting at Clones, also in Ulster. When, angrily, he said he would turn around and take another, longer route which didn't cross the border, he was told that his car would be seized. The £700 included a fine for not declaring the painting at customs. Eventually, after he'd made a number of telephone calls to Clones where local dignitaries were waiting for the painting to arrive, the Ulster Bank which commissioned the work agreed to pay the levy.[4]

Is it bloody-mindedness? The customs officers say they are just doing their job — but that has been enough to ruin many a pleasant day out for border-hopping shoppers. A number of MEPs complained when shoppers from Northern France who visited the flower fair in the Belgian border town of Mouscron found customs officers lying in wait for them on their return. They were fined nearly £70 for evading French Ministry of Agriculture plant protection regulations.

The rules state that you are not liable to pay tax on personal effects or, if you are a tradesperson, on your tools. The trouble is that customs officials don't necessarily share views about what counts as personal effects. Sometimes they rely on the rule book, which may be arbitrary or wholly out of date. Sometimes they rely on their discretion. But in any case they have the final word — not you.

The most glaring example of how customs authorities have failed to keep up with recent developments is in their attitude to personal computers. Portable they may be, but rarely across frontiers. One employee of a large multinational oil company had her £4000 IBM PC confiscated not once, but twice. Customs just wouldn't believe that an item of such value could be considered a 'personal effect'. Conservative MEP Baroness Elles has taken up one of these cases.

If face-to-face encounters with customs officials are trying, at least there is the chance of arguing your way out. You don't have that option when postal items hit the customs barrier. Any packet which is likely to fall foul of some regulation or other has to be accompanied by a description of its contents. German MEP Horst Seefeld has raised this matter with the Commission, but his effort earned little more than sympathy. Gifts frequently pose problems. If you are ever away from home for Christmas you would be well advised to tell relatives not to post your present to you. You may find it diverted to a customs warehouse miles away. And if you don't pick it up straight away, you will find yourself facing exorbitant warehousing charges. Consider what happened to a Christmas hamper sent by a Mrs Ann Radcliffe from Belgium to her uncle in Dover. It was destroyed: apparently there wasn't any space to store it. It took the uncle until the following April to find out what had happened. In the meantime customs had sent him off to get a hygiene certificate to enable him to import the meat products included in the hamper.

There has been no shortage of initiatives to curb red tape at frontiers. The introduction of green and red channels has done a great deal to speed travelling. Other technical innovations like computer readable passports and standard formats for travel documents may well help. But even when formalities are relaxed, member states still reserve the right to reintroduce them without notice. France did precisely that after a wave of terrorist bombings in 1986 in Paris. Large tailbacks developed outside French border posts, much to the annoyance of Luxembourg who retaliated by stopping every vehicle coming the other way into Luxembourg. Many felt at the time that the main purpose of the exercise was to reassure the public that the government was actually responding to the terrorist threat. I have seen no evidence that terrorists were actually caught as a result.

Other attempts to cut down border formalities have backfired badly. In 1984 France and Germany agreed that cars displaying a special green sticker on their windscreens would be allowed through customs more quickly. Within weeks of the scheme being introduced, ministries were inundated with complaints from motorists who found that customs officers were systematically stopping every other car bearing the green symbol. Despite a ringing declaration from President Mitterand of France to the effect that 'from now onwards, borders are open', the reality was that the borders were no more open than they had been before the agreement, while in some cases controls were increasing. For the ordinary traveller customs formalities are a time-consuming nuisance. But the real challenge Europe faces if it is to make the idea of a common European market a reality is how to speed up the flow of goods. For it is here that the continued existence of borders thirty years after the EEC was founded hits Europe's wallet hardest. Lord Cockfield estimates the cost to the European economy of border delays and red tape as at least $15 billion a year, equivalent to between 5 and 7 per cent of the value of goods traded annually within the European Community. It is like having a seven per cent trade tax. Even as travellers are waved through customs posts, heavy goods lorries are queueing in a separate lane with an obstacle course of formalities up ahead.

Just as the development of travel and tourism has made lengthy customs procedures for the individual politically unacceptable, so the persistence of national borders is increasingly at odds with today's economy. Trade with the rest of Europe now accounts for nearly half of Britain's output. Other European countries trade an even higher proportion of their output. It isn't just a matter of luxuries any more. Anything from ball point pens to household appliances are now shipped across national borders in huge quantities. The same brands of toothpaste, deodorant, and washing powders are on sale in every supermarket in Europe. Marks and Spencer, C&A, Benetton, Pizzaland and other chain stores can be found in city centres throughout Europe selling the same products.

It makes no sense to talk of a 'British', 'German' or 'French' car any more. Many Vauxhall cars sold in Britain are shipped in from Germany or Benelux. Even those assembled in the UK may well turn out to consist of components made in more than one

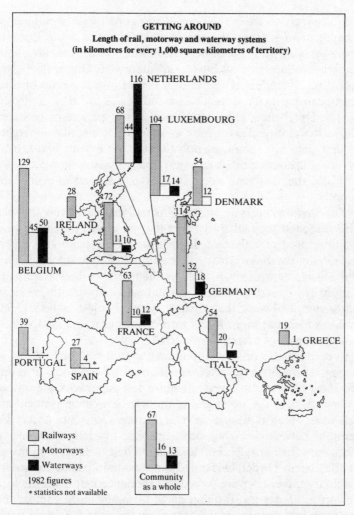

GETTING AROUND
Length of rail, motorway and waterway systems
(in kilometres for every 1,000 square kilometres of territory)

NETHERLANDS — 116

LUXEMBOURG — 104, 68, 44

129 BELGIUM, 45, 50

28 IRELAND

72 (UK), 11, 10

54 DENMARK, 17, 14, 12

114, 32, 18 GERMANY

63 FRANCE, 10, 12

39 PORTUGAL, 1, 1

27 SPAIN, 4, *

54 ITALY, 20, 7

19 GREECE, 1

Railways
Motorways
Waterways
1982 figures
* statistics not available

Community as a whole — 67, 16, 13

One example of the many irrationalities in national resistance to the internal free market: the chaotic European transport system. The European Parliament has brought the Council of Ministers to the European Court for failing to agree a truly common transport policy. The figure highlights the wildly differing levels of investment in transport in the member states.

Source: Eurostat

115

EEC country — as in the case of the Ford Fiesta mentioned in Chapter Three. Even the trucks which thunder along Europe's roads carrying these goods from one country to another are almost entirely products of joint European enterprises. One of the biggest truck manufacturers, IVECO, is a consortium made up of three European partners. Britain's Leyland trucks are now controlled by the Dutch firm DAF. A glance at any packet or container shows the reality. Take a look at a packet of biscuits, superglue, instant soup mix, paint, or polyfilla: the ingredients and instructions are in four or five languages. From a factory in Manchester or Milan they are sent out to supermarket shelves in every EEC country.

The manufacturers no longer think nationally, and few shoppers give a second thought to the fact that their biro may have been manufactured in Italy by a French-owned company and packed in German cardboard. Not so officialdom. Before they will allow the consignment through customs they have to be satisfied that nationally imposed taxes are paid and nationally determined standards complied with; that a whole statute book of national legislation, which may differ for all sorts of reasons from that operating in the country of origin, is respected.

A certificate to drive a 40 ton lorry would, you might think, be enough to qualify as an international truck driver. Sadly, it is only the most basic requirement. Patience and paperwork are at least as important at the sharp end of the war between movement and red tape which is waged daily at Europe's customs posts. The tension between drivers and customs officials exploded at Christmas time in 1984. Fed up with the delays, protesting drivers at the Italian border blockaded the mountain passes for weeks. Ordinary travellers were forced to experience first hand the lorry drivers' everyday lot. It didn't make them any more popular, but the television pictures which dominated the news for weeks finally turned the problem into a live political issue.

When this dispute flared, the average driver hauling goods from Germany to Italy needed forty separate pieces of paper. Seven documents were for the driver himself, twelve were for the load. The vehicle itself required no less than twenty-seven different pieces of paper. The protest achieved a great deal. New customs officers were appointed at undermanned posts. Formalities were simplified. working practices were improved, and border posts stayed open longer. Nevertheless, the red tape remains. Delays still average an hour at each border post, and they mount up. A lorry transporting goods from Ireland to Italy may cross six or seven borders. For all twelve EEC countries, the total number of documents required is still seventy. A document missing, or filled out incorrectly, spells trouble. Linguistic misunderstandings are another occupational hazard of the long distance lorry driver.

One tangible result of the protest was the introduction in 1987 of the Single Administrative Document, known in the trade as SAD. The idea is simple: to try and get the information required by customs onto one document. In the process, the bits of information needed were cut from 156 to 52. Nevertheless, even those items have to be gathered by the shipper and checked at every border. Even a year after its introduction drivers' unions were still somewhat sceptical. Derek Witcher of the British Road Haulage Association is not the only one to point out that the root cause of the delays is not the documents themselves but the differences in taxation and excise duty charged, in standards, in safety and health regulations which give rise to the documents in the first place. Until those go, the paperwork will stay.

Computerization could do a lot to help: indeed it is already making life easier. Ray Walker of Sitpro, who helped design the SAD, puts it neatly: 'Exporting from the UK to Brussels ought to be as easy as London to Birmingham. We need to get rid of paper — the Phoenicians started it two and a half thousand years ago. It is time for a change. A lorry could have an electronic code on the side like a big library book. The technology is in place.'

But, as he himself admits, the red tape bites downstream as well as at the border crossing. Exporters, particularly small businesses who are embarking on the adventure for the first time, are put off by the paperwork. Indeed, small businesses with little or no exporting experience could well benefit most if the Community were to do away altogether with such obstacles. The bigger international companies have learnt to live with these problems — but for them there would be cost savings.

There can be little justification for rules like the one stipulating

117

that duty must be paid if a lorry has more than 300 litres in its fuel tank. Many drivers resort to dumping fuel rather than pay up. Red tape of this kind directly induces bribery and extortion, about which few drivers are prepared to talk openly, though most admit it goes on. A 'coffee', in truckers' slang, means a bribe paid to a customs official. It isn't always so blatant, of course. The line between overzealous enforcement of some of the pettier regulations and inventing offences and pocketing the on-the-spot fine, can be very fine indeed.

Recently the Belgian authorities were forced to take action after being deluged by complaints from drivers going through Mouscron on the French border. But the game isn't only for customs officials. Drivers suspect that police on many European roads invent offences. One complained that on a recent trip through France he was fined 900 francs on the spot for speeding. The gendarme eventually settled for 150 francs in cash, which was all the driver had on him. It is not an isolated incident.

It is 8 o'clock of a windy morning on a busy Antwerp dockside. 'Long Tom' van der Mei, a 41 year old driver with years of experience on the road, is setting out with a lorry load of pears bound for Alessandro, Italy. Already he is in a queue, waiting to be issued the paperwork allowing him to leave Belgium and transit through France with his cargo. Four windows later he is informed that he can't get the necessary papers there. This is Belgium. Tom's truck is owned by a Dutch company, De Wilde. He is sent back to Holland to get his papers there . . . .

It took a further hour and a half waiting around at Dutch customs for the necessary documents to be prepared. They then discovered two documents were missing from the file. Tom was sent back to Antwerp in Belgium to pick them up. By now it was two thirty in the afternoon. And Van der Mei was still in Antwerp. Normally he would have been midway through France by the evening. But because of the late start, when he stopped for the night at 10 pm, he was only one hundred miles south of Paris, having covered that day just 378 miles. It could have been worse. The French–Belgian border turned out to be relatively hassle-free, despite its reputation for corruption.

On the next day was the open road truckers dream of, until about 3.30 pm when Van der Mei reached the spectacular Mont Blanc tunnel. The sight was uplifting. But once through, it was time to negotiate the Italian customs at Aosta. Van der Mei came down to earth with a bump. There was already a queue of vehicles from every EEC country waiting to be processed.

Then the customs post knocked off for the day. There was nothing more to be done except listen to the horror stories of other drivers. Jean-Paul Poex had been there since Wednesday of the previous week. His cargo — a truck load of fresh meat worth $25,000 — was not holding out. The Italians were insisting that the meat be tested for traces of hormones, banned under Italian law. The driver protested that the meat did not have to be tested, to no avail. They were still waiting for veterinary experts to show up to perform the tests one week later. The previous Sunday, the lorry's refrigeration unit had packed up. Poex's boss drove down that night from France in a desperate bid to save the load before it went off. It took an hour and a half to persuade the Italian bureaucracy to let the second truck into the country. Once at Aosta the customs officials allowed the meat to be transferred to the rescue truck. But now they wouldn't let either out. Both, they said, were in an 'irregular' situation.

Van der Mei was only slightly more successful. The Italians had decided they were not accepting licences to unload Belgian produce in Italy if the documents had been granted in the Netherlands. Despite arguing, pleading, begging and a series of international phone calls to company headquarters in Poeldije, Holland, they were adamant. The documents, they said, had to come from Belgium, not Holland.

He had been at Aosta for twenty-nine hours when a solution was finally agreed. The load could continue on its way but not the lorry or its driver. The final 200 miles of the journey would have to be made by Italian truck. The whole load had to be transferred at extra expense. In the end the journey of 822 miles took 62 hours, or 13 miles an hour.[5]

The barriers do not stop at the border. Officially, every EEC citizen has the right not just to move about freely but also to go and work wherever he or she wants, set up a business, exercise a profession, follow a course of study, visit a health farm or a top medical specialist — in short, to choose to live and work in any EEC country without fear of discrimination.

In practice, the right is honoured as often in the breach as in the observance. For a start, in order to be admitted one has to prove one's identity and the purpose of the visit. You then have to apply for a residence permit, usually granted by the police, for whom you are still 'an alien': they will want to see evidence that you are capable of supporting yourself. These antiquated residence laws and procedures are still based on the assumption that spending periods of one's life in other countries is a rare, not to say questionable experience. Some people simply don't bother, rather than grapple with yet another unsympathetic bureaucracy. But that solution has been known to result in deportation.

Many temporary residents, having complied with entry procedures, find themselves as Moses in Egypt, a stranger in the land. Certificates have to be presented, reasons given, questions answered. At the end of it, tax arrangements will have to be changed, driving licences exchanged, new number plates fitted on your car. You are taxed by the country in which you work but you cannot vote. Over two hundred years after the American settlers revolted against British rule under the banner of 'no taxation without representation', this is the reality for thousands of European citizens living abroad.

Abuses are far from rare. Belgium, despite being the home of the main EEC institutions, is one of the worst offenders. EEC nationals have been ordered to have their fingerprints taken or undergo medical examinations in return for what the EEC Treaty states is their birthright. The Commission is inquiring into Belgian practices after receiving complaints about delays and overchanging in the issuing of documentation.

A particularly serious case was brought to light by German MEPs. It concerned an Italian, Adolfo Ghiani, who has worked almost continuously in Nuremburg since 1960. Under EEC law, after eight years' residence a foreign visitor is entitled to turn in his or her residence permit and apply instead for 'right of abode'. However, when Signor Ghiani did so, the authorities turned down his application on 'security grounds'. Signor Ghiani was an active member of the Italian Federation for Migrant Workers which the authorities claim is controlled by the Italian Communist Party. When the MEPs took up the issue with the Commission they were given a sympathetic hearing but told that member states did have the right to curtail residence entitlements on security grounds and it was up to the government concerned to define these.[6]

Even when the security hurdle is cleared there are other restraints. One of the silliest cases to come to light was that of 100 political refugees banned from using the public baths in the small town of Dietenhofen in Bavaria. The municipal authorities claimed, in all seriousness, that foreigners were more prone to infectious diseases.

Far more serious are restrictions on opening bank accounts, buying cars, and buying shares which foreign residents regularly come up against in one country or other. Some interesting anomalies come to light. A certain M. Bode, a Luxembourger who teaches English, took on British Rail who had refused to sell him a family rail card entitling him and his family to concessionary fares. The reason? The offer only applied to UK nationals. In this case he won. After pressure from European consumer groups, British Rail agreed to change their rules. Some people have found that hospitals refuse to transfer medical records to a doctor abroad.

Getting a job can pose still more problems. Belgian football coach George Heylans had to go to the EEC Court in Luxembourg before he was allowed to join a French first division club. Others were not so lucky. A British piano teacher refused employment by an Italian school, a French journalist turned down by Belgian television and an Italian wishing to work in the British Museum library are still awaiting decisions by the Court.

For professionals, getting one's qualifications recognized may prove to be a similar headache. Doctors, architects, engineers, even plumbers have found that as far as the professional bodies are concerned the need to protect themselves comes before the interests of their clients. Apparently where you come from and where you qualified are more important than your ability to do your job.

For over twenty years the EEC has laboured to agree on

common standards for every possible trade and profession — from bakers and catering staff to nurses, hairdressers, chemists and dentists. But even these are hedged with restrictions and not always fully applied. Given the track record in getting the legislation through, it will be a long time yet before every profession is covered. It took eleven years to agree on common standards for hairdressers, eighteen years in the case of architects, and seventeen years to secure the free movement of 'self-employed persons in services incidental to transport', whatever that means.

Doctors and teachers, notably, have great difficulty moving country. In France foreign teachers can be employed in private schools, but not in the state sector. Holland decided in 1984 that the academic qualifications of Dutch nationals only would be recognized. MEP Florus Wijsenbeek made a formal complaint when he discovered that the same ministry had advised its higher educational institutes not to appoint foreigners.

What's true in theory, often turns out to be false in practice. Germany has been taken to the Court for interfering with the right of foreign orthodontists to practise. Italy, one of the worst offenders, has been censured on various occasions for laws which infringe the right of foreigners to be employed as advertising agents, journalists, chemists and tourist guides. In France, there was the case of the German artist who was barred from exhibiting his work in the chic seaside town of Biarritz. Herr Steinhauser took his case to Luxembourg, where the Court agreed that it was no use having the right to exercise one's profession freely, if one was stopped from exercising it. Auctioneers cannot practise in France either.

Getting and being allowed to keep a job is not nearly as hard as winning due consideration if one comes to live in another country for other reasons — as a French woman from Rennes who came to Britain to marry and settle in Exeter discovered to her cost. She ended up having to pay £1,914 in VAT for the furniture she brought with her, which would have been exempt had she moved for reasons other than marriage.[7]

Students are also frequently discriminated against. They are rarely barred from study abroad altogether, though this has been known to happen. Ghent University decided in September 1984, for reasons best known to itself, that it would admit only Belgian nationals to its courses in veterinary science. Belgium has been taken to the European Court on this issue and a similar one: its persistence in charging a registration fee called *minerval* for foreign students wishing to study in Belgian universities and higher education institutes. Belgium isn't the only offender. Holland has refused student grants to its own nationals studying abroad, except for those taking a limited list of agreed subjects.

Even more red tape confronts businesses which want to do business abroad. Aptly enough, the transport industry is the worst affected. Many countries insist that only their own businesses can run services, on licences which must be obtained from the national Transport Ministry. This is one of the main reasons why there are so few international coach services. West Germany charges foreign-owned coaches a special tax based on the number of kilometres they travel inside Germany territory. Many of these restrictions were originally devised to encourage the use of the railways, but nowadays they serve rather different purposes.

Take the case of the bus which ran from Frankfurt to Ostend to connect with an air shuttle to Southend airport. In 1985 the German authorities discovered that the state-run coach company Deutsche Tour was operating this highly successful service — without a licence. It stopped the service, and all attempts to obtain the licence necessary to restart it have failed. The British Conservative MP Teddy Taylor has contested the closure, which has hit not only travellers on the German side of the North Sea but also Southend airport and the company which ran the connecting bus service to London, who have no means of redress against the decision. 'Southend airport is deprived of a very remunerative service. The Miracle bus company which ferried the passengers from London to Southend is near apoplectic,' Taylor says.

The case has been taken up by British ministers, including Foreign Secretary Sir Geoffrey Howe, in numerous meetings with the Germans but to no avail. 'Surely,' the MP adds, 'a Community which requires the British people to introduce regulations controlling the noise of power lawnmowers and which spends £240 million every week on storing, dumping and destroying food surpluses is big enough to allow the Southend bus to roll across the German frontier.' Unfortunately, the answer is still no.

As things stand at the moment you would have no better luck trying to launch a ferry service or an air taxi in most European countries unless you were registered under that country's law: even then it is far from certain that necessary licences would be forthcoming.

The Commission has fought a long, hard battle with France, Germany, Denmark and Ireland over the restrictions they all impose on foreign companies wishing to sell insurance. In theory they are justified by the need to protect the consumer. But that argument does not stand up when you look at the difference between insurance premiums charged in Britain, where there is much more competition, and the exorbitant rates demanded in these countries. The EEC Court of Justice condemned Germany in December 1986 for refusing to apply a 1978 EEC Directive on co-insurance where a company spreads the risk by sharing it with other companies. Legislation covering basic personal insurance policies like home, life and car insurance is still awaited. But the Court has rejected the German argument that the only way to protect policy holders in their territory is to make sure that insurers are based there.

Similar restrictions apply to banks. It is the main reason why the high street banks cannot follow their clients abroad. Many would like to, and some banks would welcome the competition, because it would force governments which maintain strict controls on their banks to remove them. The Belgian banks, forbidden by law from fixing their own interest rates, are pushing their government to recognize that such controls can only continue because there is no competition from foreign banks. Otherwise, they would lose business to foreign banks which don't need to obey such restrictions and are therefore able to offer lower charges to their customers.

Government departments are themselves guilty of discrimination. As major consumers of goods and services, they nearly all operate policies which restrict public purchasing to national companies. Goods produced in every sector of the economy are affected, from radiators for heating public buildings to school books and multi-million printing contracts for all that paperwork: from paperclips and ball point pens for the pen-pushers to equipment for the army, computers, buses and railway carriages. Imagine how many plastic dustbins the British civil service uses . . . how much furniture . . . food for canteens . . . hospital equipment and drugs. For almost every project you can think of, government is the biggest customer, accounting for as much as 20 per cent of all goods and services traded in the economy.

Governments are obviously eager to ensure that national companies and employees benefit first from the public sector's huge spending power. But this may be shortsighted. In many cases it means less value for money, not more. Companies enjoying 'contracts for life' have no incentive to increase their efficiency and are often able to set their own prices, a privilege bitterly resented by other businesses which have to compete hard for markets. The public ends up getting less and paying more — an estimated $400 billion more in the EEC as a whole every year. Proponents of the single internal market argue that such policies have another, longer term side effect. As each country favours its own national companies, in some key sectors Europe ends up with twelve small competing companies, none of which is able to compete with American giants on its own.

Nowhere is this truer than in telecommunications, though examples abound in everything from the steel industry to airlines, currently a symbol of national identity rivalling an army, a police force and postage stamps. All European countries operate a telecommunications monopoly, and all (except Britain since British Telecom was privatized) are state-owned. Together they invest some £14 billion a year. But (again with the exception of Britain) they all spend that money on national equipment suppliers. While each national industry makes comfortable profits, collectively the European industry is being left behind in the rush for new world markets. Instead of concentrating their efforts on beating off the stiff competition from America and Japan, they are fighting with each other. The result is that while the North American industry has come up with just four rival versions of digital switching systems, which telecom companies are using to replace the creaking manual exchanges in preparation for the 1990s, Europe has eleven different systems on offer.

The current £1 billion EEC surplus in telecommunications products could be wiped out by the end of the decade, according to UNICE, the European employers' federation. For an industry which will be at the forefront of the information technology revolution, and which could be accounting for 7 per cent of European gross domestic product by the year 2000 — compared with 3 per cent now — this could be nothing short of catastrophic.

Very similar considerations lie behind the move to sweep away restrictions in the financial markets. Internal market theorists believe that until Europeans develop a financial market of their own — by removing national barriers to trade in securities and other financial instruments — Europe will remain dependent on the Wall Street roller coaster. The former French Finance Minister and current President of the European Commission, Jacques Delors, cites the stock exchange crash in October 1987, when Wall Street triggered an imitative collapse in Europe's capital markets, to illustrate the urgent need for a single European market.

One of the toughest obstacles to the removal of trade barriers in Europe is the disparity of national standards. That British plugs will not fit European sockets is only the sign of more fundamental incompatibilities, invisible barriers which are hard to define, easy to defend and as costly to change as they are to maintain. Inevitably, they present the doubters with their easiest target.

Much fun has been had at the expense of the bureaucrats who worked for years to achieve common standards for sausages and lawnmowers. But as long as failure to meet national standards can be used as a bar to imports, manufacturers have a real headache. If the British are happy to eat chocolate with a higher proportion of fat and less cocoa than the French, that is fine for them. But it makes it very hard for a British company wishing to export chocolate to France.

There are some laughable examples of the use of discrepant standards to bar imports. Take the case of the Danish government's refusal to allow foreign brewers to export canned beer to Denmark, despite the fact that its own famous lager is widely exported in cans — to the tune of 250 million a year. Denmark says the reason is environmental. Brewers are obliged to sell beer in returnable bottles of types approved by government legislation. Inevitably, it is harder for foreign bottlers to meet these standards and operate bottle return systems.

Another proud beer-drinking nation, the Germans, were forced to drop an age old law widely used to bar foreign beer. Known as the *reinheitsgebot*, the law dated back to 1516 and forbade the use of additives, insisting on the use of the traditional ingredients only: barley, water, malt, hops and yeast. The case provides a wonderful example of the specious arguments often used to justify such restrictions. The West German government's lawyer argued that in a country where the average annual consumption of beer is 148 litres per head, the state is right to protect its drinkers from a dangerous build-up of chemical additives. Full marks to the West German consumers' association: it congratulated the Court of Justice when Luxembourg backed the Commission's claim that what is good enough for everyone else is good enough for the Germans, too. A spokesman pointed out that 'The only ingredient in domestic and foreign beer that has so far been proven to be potentially damaging is alcohol.' The government's case was also undermined, it must be said, by the fact that its professed concern did not extend to the health of non-Germans. The German beer exported to Britain or France contains as many additives as any other.

This was the second major case of its kind that the Germans lost. Commission lawyers had established an important precedent when Germany was censured by the Luxembourg court for banning import of the French liqueur Cassis because it did not contain enough alcohol. The court ruled conclusively that what is good enough for the French should be good enough for the Germans and vice versa.

However ridiculous those arguments may seem, they demonstrate the difficulties raised by the issue of standards. The huge German brewing industry obviously had a vested interest in maintaining the *reinheitsgebot*. But for many Germans the quality of their beer is an emotive issue. They believe they are fully entitled to demand high standards for their national drink even if the

French are happy to drink beer brewed from rice. National preoccupations do differ, and national standards reflect this.

Nothing illustrates that better than the debate about pollution standards for cars. Working to a separate standard for each country is proving increasingly costly for manufacturers who have to produce different models to meet the various specifications. But when ministers and civil servants sit down to negotiate a set of common standards, national differences prove astonishingly difficult to resolve. Britain tends not to worry too much about pollution. For the Danes and Germans it is a major political issue.

The Commission wants to see the Cassis principle applied across the board. It sees no reason why anything which can be sold in one country should not be sold in another, provided certain minimum standards are observed. Where there are wide differences of opinion, the consumer should be king. Clear labelling on foodstuffs, for instance, should ensure that the shopper is able to exercise a choice.

Simple as that sounds, in practice many consumers are bewildered by labelling. Unless they've been warned off a specific additive, as sufferers from particular allergies, few people are in a position to weigh up the scientific information themselves. Without proper controls manufacturers can abuse terms like 'natural' and 'wholesome'. If national authorities cease to impose trading standards for fear of red tape and covert protectionism, it is difficult to see who will.

Clearly, labelling cannot be a substitute for specific safety standards when it comes to products such as electrical appliances, cars, toys, machinery or drugs. But it is precisely these standards which generate the most red tape and the most impenetrable barriers. Every new car, every new household iron must pass separate tests in each EEC country before it is put on the market. In many cases different models have to be made in order to meet the various standards demanded.

The Volvo plant in Ghent, Belgium, produces trucks for sale throughout Europe. In order to meet the requirements laid down in all EEC countries, it has to make eight separate basic models and eighty-four different versions; it must also provide 235 separate certificates. When a truck is exported to France the airbrakes have to be sent on ahead, ostensibly for individual examination.

Similar examples can be cited in practically every sector of industry. The application of national standards is fertile ground for Catch-22 situations. When West Germany decided to liberalize telecommunications and allow foreign firms to supply telephone equipment, it left the power to set and approve standards in the hands of the German post office, the Bundespost. In more than one case the temptation not to approve a rival make of telephone proved too strong. Foreign telecommunications equipment suppliers could not sell their equipment in Germany without Bundespost approval and the Bundespost was not giving it.

Even when it is not quite as blatant as that, national standards authorities have always been tempted to go for standards their own industry favours. The argument over whether catalytic converters, which filter out poisonous exhaust gases, or so-called lean burn engines, which burn fuel more efficiently and give off less toxic gas, were the best way of limiting car pollution had less to do with science and more to do with the fact that Ford UK had already taken a lead in the development of lean burn technology when the issue of car exhaust pollution came up before the EEC's Council of Ministers.

Such tactics can backfire. In the early days of colour television, France adopted the Secam colour TV system to protect its national TV manufacturers. When everyone else opted for the rival Pal system they were left high and dry. By the time the EEC began to discuss compatible standards for satellite TV France had learnt its lesson. Britain may find itself forced to abandon three point plugs for similar reasons.

As information technology reaches into every aspect of life, the whole issue of standardization is taking on a new importance. Standards are not just a matter of whether the sale of a product is within the law. They also affect whether it will work. Just as with television, where the decoder in the TV set has to be able to understand the signals it receives, so also with computer programmes, video recorders and cassette tapes.

Unless standards are agreed throughout Europe — still a distant goal — a growing range of vital everyday equipment simply will not work. We are now looking forward to an age where data exchange networks — for example, electronic banking systems which allow people to withdraw cash from automatic machines twenty-four hours a day — are assuming increasing importance. Banks are finding it very difficult to set up a common European system enabling, say, French customers to withdraw money in Germany, because the networks have grown up autonomously. They have developed their own systems which cannot readily understand each other.

Computers are increasingly using the public telephone network to exchange information. Again, they can only do so if everyone can agree on what system is used for converting the information into signals which can be sent down a telephone line without interfering with ordinary telephone communications.

This is the infrastructure of the future. Yet telecommunications and standards authorities are all organized on national lines, banking systems are based on national legislation, and governments are way behind in technological thinking: it is little wonder, then, that Europe is so far from setting up advanced systems which cross national borders. Priority is still given to systems which work within their own national boundaries. EEC member states continue to believe that by adopting their own standards they can give their national champions a head start when it comes to negotiating international standards. Such thinking is proving increasingly short-sighted. The price of a fragmented market is a high one, and getting higher as development costs mount. Trying to maintain obsolescent standards nationally only increases the eventual cost once everyone has to fall into line.

Unnecessary controls, delays, red tape and incompatible standards all increase costs and impair a national industrial base in an increasingly international climate. In addition to wasted effort, lost time and superfluous employment on unproductive paperwork, there are other unseen and unmeasurable costs.

Not least of these is the hassle factor, which discourages people from doing what they ought to be able to do by right. But there is also the unseen cost of a Europe divided into separate, almost watertight economic compartments. This is what prevents the region from mobilizing its 320 million inhabitants in the pursuit of common economic goals — while the United States, with a smaller population, uses its home market as a springboard from which to dominate markets abroad. If 200 million Americans can support a space programme, the world's biggest aerospace contractor, and the world's leading computer, telecommunications equipment and electronics firms, is there any reason why a united Europe should not be able to do the same?

Free market evangelists insist that this continued 'Balkanization' of Europe's internal market also prevents the advantages of technological advance and greater efficiency from reaching all the European Community's inhabitants. Consumer groups, however, argue that far from bringing down the barriers many companies actually find that they can benefit from the existence of twelve different European markets, playing one off against the other at the ordinary consumer's expense.

How come walkmen cost more than twice as much in Denmark as in the UK? Why are compact discs nearly 50 per cent more expensive in France than in Britain? Only, consumer groups claim, because the consumer market in Europe is still broken up into national compartments. A survey by the European Bureau of Consumer Unions, which brings together consumer organizations from all Community countries, showed in 1987 that the same package holiday to the Hotel las Ocas in Benidorm, Spain, cost nearly twice as much when booked through Touropa in Paris as when booked through Thomson UK in Britain. 'Such price differences,' the survey concludes, 'cannot be explained by external factors alone, and reflect the insulation of national markets by the travel industry.'[8]

Similarly startling findings have emerged from surveys comparing differences in the prices of computers and cars. Whilst Britain is one of the cheapest countries for purchasing electronic products, the main car manufacturers have known for years that the British will pay more for their cars than other Europeans. They were even prepared to go to the extent of banning personal imports, until their attempts to stop Britons buying right-hand drive cars more cheaply through dealers in Belgium were frustrated by the European Commission.

The case for removing the remaining barriers to free trade and free movement of capital in Europe undoubtedly rests on some highly controversial and contested assumptions. Studies of the economic cost of a fragmented European market greatly outnumber projections of the wider social and economic costs of a free market. What would be the hidden costs of a further concentration of economic activity in a diminishing heartland region of the European Community? How should the loss of jobs and investment opportunities in the weaker and less viable regions of the European Community be costed?

The socio-economic balance sheet of completing the internal market is certain to be at the heart of European Community politics between now and 1992 — when the last of the barriers is due to disappear. The outcome will depend to a large extent on the economic background against which the key decisions will be taken over the next few years.

The most favourable background would obviously be one of economic growth and an optimistic business environment. Conversely, renewed recession and persistent and even increasing unemployment may challenge some of the assumptions behind the internal market case. In the 1980s the argument on trade and capital movement liberalization was won hands down by the liberalizers — on the grounds of freedom, choice and efficiency. It is open to question whether they will have the argument all their own way in the years ahead.

6
The End of the Old
Industrial Order in Europe

From its inception the European Community — 'The Common Market' — has been concerned chiefly with economic, commercial and industrial matters. Indeed until recent years the correct designation for the Common Market was 'the European Economic Communities', as if to emphasize economic issues over the political, social and other questions dealt with in the Treaty of Rome.

The six founder member states came together in the mid-1950s precisely in order to integrate their economies, stimulate economic growth and international trade, and so underpin mass employment and rising living standards. In the early 1950s most Western European countries were still living in the shadow of the decades of poverty and mass unemployment which had preceded the Second World War.

In the first ten years after 1945 there was little confidence that the post-war economic recovery could be guaranteed in the longer term. Parallels were frequently drawn with the years after the First World War when an economic boom gave way by the mid-1920s to recession and, ultimately, the depression.

The first and most important Western strategy to avert a repetition was Marshall Aid, adopted by the Truman Administration in 1947. This undoubtedly prevented something close to financial collapse in a number of West European economies in the late 1940s. The spectre which the Truman Administration invoked to persuade a suspicious and reluctant US Congress was that of financial collapse rapidly followed by a 'Communist takeover' in countries such as France and Italy.[1] Although the strength of the West European Communist Parties was grossly exaggerated, there is no doubt that the existence of mass Communist parties at that time, combined with the worsening Cold War after the Berlin crisis and Stalin's Czech coup of 1948, generated the necessary political will in the US to provide the aid that put the West European economies on a recovery course. Of course, it soon became apparent that by assisting this recovery Marshall Aid was creating important export markets for US firms.

By the early 1950s, policy makers in Western Europe were convinced that without some bold step the impetus provided by Marshall Aid and the indirect stimulus given by the Korean War would peter out. This reasoning led to the creation of the European Coal and Steel Community in 1950 and motivated Monnet and Schuman to pursue the goal of a wider European Economic Community in the years which followed.

As we have noted, the Treaty of Rome deals primarily with economic and commercial issues. However the unwritten assumption is that the Treaty and the European Community have their ultimate justification in the social goal of continued economic advance and full employment.[2]

Indeed, as the 1950s passed, it became more and more unthinkable that the countries of the European Community — and later the rival European Free Trade Association — would ever willingly permit or tolerate a return to mass unemployment and the interruption of economic growth. The most pressing problems of economic policy appeared to lie in the sphere of distribution rather than production. The first doubts about the durability of economic expansion emerged during the late 1960s and early 1970s: the dollar crises in the United States, the subsequent OPEC oil price increase of 1973, and the global inflation and recession which followed.

In retrospect it is clear that, quite apart from the return to instability and more volatile trade cycles, some of the European Community's most important industrial sectors were experiencing deepening problems of structural obsolescence and a dramatic decline in international competitiveness. European industry was losing its share of world export markets not only to Japan, but also to the newly industrialized countries of the Pacific Rim.

The 1970s also saw a dramatic expansion in the productive

capacity of industries such as steel, textiles and shipbuilding in many of the new industrialized countries, not only in the Far East, but also in parts of Latin America. Large, integrated and technologically advanced plants in these countries added, however, to the developing problem of global overcapacity. This was clearly revealed by the world recession of the mid 1970s and the even more acute economic downturn of the early 1980s.

Quite suddenly, or so it seemed, the European Community faced a major employment crisis. Many of its heavy industries experienced contraction and near collapse, and that took the wind out of the sails of full employment. The results were devastating for those who were directly affected and for whole regions of the European Community that depended on these industries. For the first time, confidence in the ability of European governments to maintain full employment began to weaken. The break with past policy assumptions was underlined when, from the early 1980s, the emphasis of government policies in the European Community switched from a Keynesian preoccupation with job creation and fiscal expansion to an all-out attempt to curb monetary growth and inflation and reduce public sector spending. The right-of-centre 'monetarist' governments elected during this period saw the use of public expenditure to 'pump prime' economic activity as the root cause of economic decline in the productive sectors of European economies.

Just as regions in the North of England, Scotland and Wales, or Wallonia in Belgium, Lorraine in France and the Ruhr in Germany were facing the gravest post-war employment crisis, they were confronted by national governments for whom full employment and interventionist policies to stimulate investment were not a priority. For a generation of Europeans growing to adulthood in the late 1980s, heavy industry and mass industrial employment were things they learned about from history books rather than through their own life experiences. The decline of steel, coal, shipbuilding and textiles have a lot in common. They also have distinctive features to which planners in the European Community have had to respond.

135

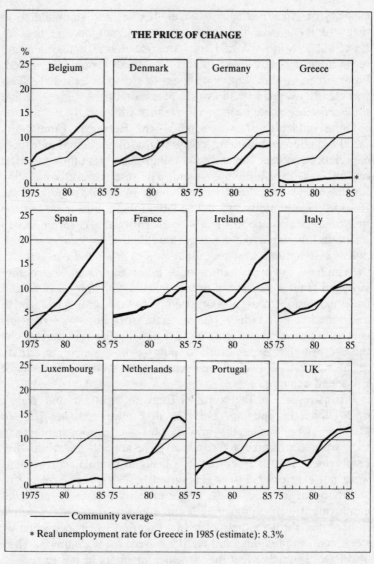

THE PRICE OF CHANGE

Unemployment trends in the member countries (registered unemployed only). The Community average is still well over 10 per cent.

Source: Eurostat

The Disappearing World of Industrial Employment

The concrete and glass palace which houses the European Commission's Brussels headquarters is a monument to the slide rule technocracy which made its home there in the heyday of the Sixties. Now that slide rules have given way to computer workstations and databases, it looks as dated as the vision of the future which fired its original occupants.

Then, technology meant cars, transistors and aeroplanes. Now Euro-strategists are looking to laser optics and information technologies to provide the wealth — and the jobs — on which Europe's future depends. But there is another side to the coin. While those who are planning that radiant future view it with an understandable excitement, the transition to a high tech and service-based economy is going to mean profound changes in the way people earn their living, and in society as a whole. There is a price to be paid. Smokestack industries were once the powerhouse of the European economy. Now they are seen by most planners as an albatross around its neck. But if they are to go, there will be losers. Many communities, many millions of people depended on them. They are being asked to trade their livelihoods against a promise of future prosperity. The new jobs will not necessarily be the same jobs, or in the same places, or even in the same numbers. It is a price which is being paid now, by millions of people who are in the frontline.

Europe's wealth was built on the reserves of coal and iron ore which fuelled the industrial revolution. They provided the power and machinery which transformed the textile and shipbuilding trades into manufacturing industries. Even when cars and electrical goods took their place as the locomotive industries of the postwar European economy, coal and steel were still the foundations of economic prosperity.

The European Coal and Steel Community was established in 1951. Though the post-war Labour government saw these as the 'commanding heights' of the economy, it reasoned that under European control they would be a force for wider economic cooperation. The mighty coal and steel basin of the Ruhr, which had fuelled Hitler's armies could be harnessed for peace.

When, as they had foreseen, the Coal and Steel Community led to the European Economic Community itself in 1958, coal and steel kept their pre-eminence. The European Commission maintained a degree of control over these industries which has never been applied to any others. Now, of course, those powers are used for precisely the opposite purpose to that intended by the founders: to manage the orderly running-down of the industries they once sustained.

Once, industry's demand for steel was insatiable. Cars, 'white goods', and pipelines all consumed huge quantities of steel. Maintaining record levels of steel output was the key to economic growth. Steel mills in turn needed coking coal, usually supplied by nearby mines, to keep the furnaces going.

As the economic boom gathered pace, steel output continued to grow. New, more efficient plants came on stream. By 1970 output was at record levels. New processes and economies of scale meant more steel could be produced by fewer workers. In 1945 nearly half a million people were employed in making steel in Britain. By 1970 a workforce half the size was producing three times as much steel. Efficiency and rising demand meant profits for most European steel producers. A healthy economic climate meant there were plenty of other skilled manual jobs for displaced steelworkers. At its peak in 1974, production reached 156 million tonnes.

Recession put paid to the rapid growth. Almost overnight demand slumped as the car and white goods industries were hit by the economic squeeze and Japanese imports. The car industry which once took 2 million tonnes of steel now takes a third of that. The shipbuilding industry, once the largest single customer, needs less than 47,000 tonnes when once it was taking 650,000 tonnes. Britain now produces half the steel it was making in 1970, with a workforce five times smaller.

The same story has been repeated right across Europe. Germany is Europe's biggest steel producer and the fifth largest in the world. Until the mid-1980s its 200,000 employees brought in huge profits. No longer. The car industry shrank and the American market, once a major outlet for German steel, is now virtually closed. In the 1970s, 130,000 German steelworkers left the industry for jobs elsewhere. Now their prospects of reemployment are bleak: the growth rate of the West German economy is one of the most sluggish in Europe. Italy, which leapt into sixth place in the league table of steel producers, increasing output and employment whilst others cut back, is now having to scale down production.

There are those who argue that the answer lies in a change in economic policy. A concerted push for growth would get demand going and rekindle the dying furnace fires. But that seems very optimistic: far-reaching changes have taken place that are unlikely to be reversed.

A return to 1970s levels of demand for steel is highly unlikely. Even if growth is restored, the economy has changed: in the 1990s and beyond, growth will not come from those industries which in the past consumed vast quantities of steel. That has gone forever. And even those industries are changing. Tougher plastics, new materials and aluminium have pushed steel off its pedestal. Industry also uses raw materials far more efficiently. In 1960 it took 1.1 tonnes of steel to make the average car. Already it takes half that, and by the year 2000 the figure could halve again.

Cheap steel is also flooding in from the new industrial countries of Asia, with lower overheads and cheaper labour costs — achieved, it is often forgotten, by draconian labour laws which suppress trade union militancy. Brazil, Korea and Taiwan undercut European producers in their domestic markets; they are eating away at the export markets, too.

When the crisis struck, European steelmakers were in sight of an output of 200 million tonnes a year. They were in for a shock. From the 1974 peak of 156 million tonnes, production steadily fell to a level of about 115 million tonnes in the mid-1980s. Consumption fell by a fifth and prices collapsed even more spectacularly: by 45 per cent between 1974 and 1977.

In 1980, with overcapacity approaching fifty per cent, the Commission decided to intervene. Using the exceptional powers mentioned above, the industry commissioner Viscount Etienne Davignon put together the rescue plan which was later to bear his name. Put simply, the plan offered steelmakers a breathing space to put their house in order. The Commission offered production quotas, guaranteed minimum prices, and import controls. In return, steelmakers would have to deliver the necessary plant closures to remove the chronic overcapacity which was depressing prices and costing European taxpayers millions of marks, pounds and francs to maintain. They failed, in the main, to honour their side of the bargain. In 1983 the steel industry was operating at the staggeringly low level of 57 per cent capacity, nowhere near the 80 per cent target fixed by Davignon.

Cheating was widespread. While British Steel slashed production capacity, the Italians actually produced more. Employment in Britain halved — from 162,000 to 84,000. But combined steel employment in France, West Germany and Italy fell from 427,000 to 375,000, a much smaller cut. Davignon himself complained of a fraud called 'seconds'. New steel was deliberately damaged so as to be reclassified as seconds, which were not subject to price controls. In 1983 Klöckner of West Germany deliberately outproduced its quota, ignoring fines imposed by the European Commission.

But the worst offenders were governments, who continued to sanction the subsidies necessary to keep plants open. Despite the restrictions, EEC governments forked out £20.4 billion during the lifetime of the Davignon plan to finance the steel industry. In 1985 Karl-Heinz Narjes, who took over from Davignon, managed to push through what by then seemed to the Commission the only answer: a total ban on operational aid from governments. As a result 50 million tonnes worth of capacity went and with it 125,000 jobs.

By 1986 some controls had been removed. Only 60 per cent of the industry's output was covered by ECSC regulation, compared with 85 per cent at the height of the Davignon plan. The industry was running at 70 per cent capacity, better than at the height of the crisis, but still sufficiently short of the 80 per cent target to cause continued concern. Profitability was returning to the industry, too. But there was considerable doubt about its ability to cope without controls. Regulation had managed to keep prices up, after the catastrophic slide in the late seventies. Now the Commission was pushing for the blanket removal of controls which seemed to be stringing out the inevitable process of shutting down surplus capacity, rather than speeding it up as originally had been hoped.[3]

As in the case of agriculture, interventionist policies create their own dependent lobby. When plans were mooted to remove controls altogether by the end of 1987, the main steel producers protested. Sheltering behind the European steel federation, Eurofer, they appealed for quotas to stay in return for one more chance to organize their own capacity reductions. With over-capacity still high, they feared a repeat of the collapse in steel prices which had been so damaging to the industry in the seventies.

Independent consultants Peat Marwick were commissioned to carry out a confidential survey of steelmakers to discover what potential there was for a voluntary closure plan. After visiting no less than 35 plants, they came back with a report recommending that 15 million tonnes of capacity could be scrapped, in return for maintaining controls, particularly on imports, plus an unspecified sum in compensation. This fell a long way short of the Commission's own estimate of surplus capacity which was in the region of 30 million tonnes. But the biggest shortcoming, from the Commission's point of view, was a lack of willingness on the part of steelmakers to offer major cuts in the most critical area of all — that of hot rolled coil, the sheet steel used for making cars and white goods. This is the product which has suffered the severest slump in demand. It is mainly produced in big integrated steelworks, often located in areas of industrial decline (in some cases the car and white goods factories they service have long left the area) where closure would cause the greatest hardship. Here lies the crux of the whole debate. Closing plants like the Sacilor-Usinor hot rolled plants at Sollac or Dunkirk in France, or Raven-scraig in Scotland, are political decisions. The fates of communities cannot rest on economic criteria alone.

Commissioner Narjes told steelmakers that the equivalent of five integrated plants would have to go if the industry was to return to profitability by 1990. That would cost a further 22,000 jobs on top of the 125,000 lost between 1980 and 1985. When other necessary steel cuts were included, the cost of returning to profitability was put at a minimum of 80,000 job losses, at a time when average unemployment was hovering around 11 per cent. There were little grounds for supposing it would come down soon.[4]

Was there any alternative to more cuts? Ken Collins, MEP for the Scottish constituency which included the Ravenscraig plant, could point to the contradiction between the Brussels Commission's economic strategy, which called for more growth, and its plans for the steel industry which meant further contraction. But it is hard to see how the economy of the future is going to use even the steel which is being produced now.

A slight recovery in mid-1987 led German steelmakers to protest that the Commission's forecasts were excessively gloomy. They were looking over their shoulders at the Italians whom they blamed for most of their difficulties. Once again the need for European solidarity was underscored. Unless everyone was confident that everyone else was pulling their weight — bearing their fair share of closures — the strategy would collapse in a scramble from which no one would emerge unscathed. Europe's taxpayers would foot the bill for subsidies and backdoor deals which failed to restore the industry's health or avert major job losses. What Brussels was constantly trying to avoid was a subsidies war.

Even among the Germans there was little real optimism about the future. Indeed, many argued that it was a myth to assume that the industry could be turned around merely by cutting back enough. Dr Heinz Kriwet, chairman of Thyssen Stahl, warned that no one knew what degree of overcapacity remained in the industry. Others urged abandonment of the belief that somehow the industry could be returned to profitability without public support. Some degree of subsidy was inevitable. Indeed, Gerhard Cromme of Krupp attacked his government for not supporting its own industry enough.

Yet traditionally, the efficient West German steel industry has been the most sceptical about the Community's interventionist approach on production quotas and minimum prices. That point of view was forcefully put by the executive director of the German Iron and Steel Federation, Dr Ruprecht Von Dran. 'We believe in free trade and we are sorry that the Treaty establishing the European Coal and Steel Community had dirigistic as well as

142

liberal elements — they have been existing side by side. For thirty years we made use of the liberal free market clauses in the ECSC Treaty. But since 1980 we have had an interventionist, dirigist system in Europe.'

Dr Von Dran said that his federation hoped to get rid of this system 'as soon as possible', adding that he meant as soon as there were no longer any national subsidies for steel production 'which distort international competition'. This pure gospel of a free market in steel is not of course advocated so forcefully by the older, integrated steel plants in the Ruhr as it is by the representatives of the more modern and competitive southern steel plants.

There are signs that in the Ruhr in particular anger at the run down of surplus steelmaking capacity is reaching boiling point. This was given dramatic expression in the winter of 1987 when news of a further threatened loss of 400,000 steel jobs — mainly in the Ruhr — was followed by a week of angry and violent demonstrations and plant occupations by German steel workers, with the support of the trade unions and their local communities.

British Steel's return to profitability in 1987 reinforced chairman Bob Scholey's view that the corporation had emerged from restructuring in better shape than its continental rivals. It was a remarkable turn-around for a nationalized industry which once seemed to typify the lame duck, loss-making image of the British public sector. Once in the red to the tune of £1 million a day, it was now a surefire candidate for privatization.

Officially, BSC was straining at the leash, complaining that having to pay rivals £45 per tonne for their production quotas was an unfair burden. But that view underestimated the extent to which the controls in place since 1980 had contributed to BSC's spectacular recovery by stabilizing the market. True, British Steel had gone further than its continental rivals in scrapping capacity to meet the requirements of the Davignon plan. But the removal of controls would, if coupled with a failure of the German and Italian steel industry to 'bite the bullet' (as Norman Tebbit phrased it when industry minister), leave British Steel with a dilemma: whether to pursue a predatory pricing policy in a buyers' market — a high risk strategy — or to throw in its lot with others in the industry, setting up a cartel of some kind to minimize the damage scrapping quotas threatened to cause.

Either way, a further deterioration in market conditions would throw all calculations of profit into the melting pot. Many hoped — not least among them Industry Commissioner Karl-Heinz Narjes and Kenneth Clarke, Tebbit's successor — that removing the remaining controls would mean that further closures would be enforced by the dictates of the market, not by governments or Brussels. Politicians would be relieved of the burden of having to take decisions which should have been left to the managers. In this view, political interference had distorted steel policy from the start, making it harder to achieve a rational strategy.

Outdated plant would have been scrapped earlier, money would not have been wasted in building new steel mills for which there was no market, or on subsidies to prop up plants which could never hope to be profitable. Hopes were built up which could not be sustained. The pain was strung out, not softened. The money would have been better spent elsewhere, either on industries with a more promising future or in developing special steels in which European firms could find a niche safe from foreign competition.

This view received a great deal of support among consumers of steel. Under the quota system they face what is in effect an officially sanctioned cartel. Even products which are not covered by the quotas, or are outside the framework of the Coal and Steel Treaty, are affected: the approach tends to spill over. The chemical, food processing and catering equipment industries are major buyers of stainless steel. They complain at the frequent price increases over which they have no control. It is an open secret that these prices are fixed by the Sendzimin club — or Z club for short — named after the inventor of the stainless steel process. When buyers went elsewhere for cheaper quotes they were told that suppliers were unable to comply. Practices such as these have aroused the suspicions of the Commission's competition directorate.

The main steel producers, many of whom are nationalized and almost all of whom are dependent on some degree of state support, often seem to outsiders to have far too much clout for their own good. Independent steel producers have been understandably resentful that they were not playing by the same rules. Customers want cheaper steel, and economists argue that this would cut costs for industry as a whole. A policy which regulates the market merely strengthens the appeal of substitute products or cheaper imported supplies.

Political considerations, have prevailed however. Despite the declining importance of steel in the new economy which began taking shape in the 1980s, many people still believed that to allow market forces to determine steelmaking capacity was to jettison all faith in Europe's future as a manufacturing centre. There was also the human factor. Steel had always been a major employer. Many plants were located in regions suffering from the implosion of traditional manufacturing industries. Coal, steel, shipbuilding, textile, engineering and later car industries were often intertwined and located in close proximity. When one went so did the rest, eventually. Steelworkers had accepted job losses over the years, in return for a more efficient industry and enhanced job security for those who stayed. But promises that plant closures would leave a more healthy industry behind proved impossible to guarantee, and in the end were no longer believed. Despite the closures, the situation continued to deteriorate. Five years after one closure plan had been completed, they were facing a further wave of shutdowns. How long could this go on without the European steel industry disappearing altogether?

The human cost of running down the steel industry rarely entered into the equation. Steelworkers were told that money consigned to the bottomless pit of doomed steel plants would be better spent creating jobs with a future. The European Commission argued that subsidies should support new investment in the areas where traditional employers were in decline. But it signally lacked the resources to finance programmes that would make an impact. The Resider programme which the Commission proposed to accompany the next stage of steel restructuring was costed in millions of pounds when it should have been costed in billions. Previous experience of job creation suggests that to create one manufacturing job costs hundreds of thousands of pounds.

There has been little evidence, either, that national governments are ready to step into the breach. BSC Industries Ltd, a company set up to create jobs to replace those lost in steel areas, spent some £13 million. Even according to its own figures, it helped to create no more than 65,000 jobs. And such calculations are notoriously unreliable. It is impossible to say whether some of those would not have existed anyway.

Few of the steel towns have recovered from closure. Shotton, Scunthorpe, Consett seem condemned to permanently high levels of unemployment. Morale is low. Redundancy pay helped cushion the immediate blow, but it has virtually all gone. Only a handful of people were able to use the money to set up their own businesses.

What money there was for those areas often went to finance projects of questionable value. In Corby, the European Commission and the European Investment Bank together stumped up part of the money to help build a new entertainments and recreation park. In employment terms it was a mere drop in a huge ocean of joblessness. To many people in Corby, with plenty of enforced leisure but little money to spend, the choice betrayed an astonishing lack of sensitivity.

Governments were more than happy to let the Commission take the blame for policies they dictated. When the jobs went they pointed the finger at Brussels, whilst starving it of the funds needed to make a job replacement programme feasible. Plans to double the EEC's regional and social funds from their absurdly low level of six per cent of the total EEC budget in 1987 were bitterly resisted by precisely those countries in which the social effects of industrial decline were most glaring. Most of that increase was destined to go to Spain and Portugal, countries which joined the Community in 1986. Rather than allow such an increase to go ahead, Britain and Germany preferred to deprive their own declining industrial regions of EEC assistance.

Steelyard Blues

Maxhütte

Salzbach-Rosenberg is a town where steel making has a long tradition. It has been produced here since 1853, until recently from locally mined ore, and has provided employment for generations of the town's menfolk. Today the Maxhütte steel works dominates Salzbach-Rosenberg physically and economically. It is the largest single employer in the town, and in the whole region of Oberpfalz, which though part of the rich state of Bavaria is one of the poorest areas in Germany.

The plant has been under threat for some years now. In April 1987 Maxhütte's owners, Klöckner, put the plant into receivership. It is now the focus of a mass campaign involving the union IG Metall and local, mainly social democrat (SPD) councillors. They are fighting a highly conservative state government which is dominated by Franz-Josef Strauss's Christian Social Union and a management which seems to have little faith in the plant. Many believe the trouble dates from 1977 when Klöckner bought the plant off Flick. Klöckner, who have large steel interests throughout Germany, are suspected locally of having planned to run the plant down from the start. They were accused at the time they took over Maxhütte of aiming to eliminate competition and engage in an asset stripping operation.

Little that has happened since has disproved the charge. Production was been located elsewhere. Management were accused of using transfer pricing fiddles to make Maxhütte look uneconomic. Klöckner have already tried to close the plant once but were stopped by a mass demonstration. That did not stop the slower, inexorable seeping away of jobs. The cold rolled plant was closed and the work transferred to Bremen at the cost of 700 jobs. In 1983, the older men at the works were offered a guarantee of no loss of earnings if they took early retirement. Over a thousand took advantage of the offer.

Maxhütte's case is not strong. Salzbach-Rosenberg no longer makes economic sense as a steel production centre. Oberpfalz's main pre-war customers lay in East Germany. Delivery costs now exceed those of steel plants located in northern Germany, where Klöckner is seeking to transfer production. Iron ore is no longer produced locally since a nearby mine closed with the loss of 283 jobs. There is still plenty of ore under the ground, but it is cheaper to import from Australia even though there is no local port to take delivery of this ore. The plant's small size also works against it.

147

The local drama has been played out against a wider canvas of factors which neither workforce nor management can control. Klöckner complained that EEC quotas had made the works unprofitable. In 1981 it was producing 1.4 million tonnes of crude steel a year, but output was down to 0.9 million tonnes when the company was put into receivership, a drop of 40 per cent. A quarter of Maxhütte's output was covered by the EEC quotas. Of the five conveyor belts for steel sections only three were in use.

The workers were angry at what they saw as unfair foreign competition, particularly the practice of taking scrap metal from southern Germany to be smelted down in Italy for reimportation as steel for reinforcing concrete, one of Maxhütte's products. Ironically, the Bavarian plant does much the same with Russian scrap, imported by Klöckner's scrap metal subsidiary.

Nevertheless, the plant is not without prospects. Although poorly placed to supply the domestic German market, it is in a better position to benefit from an expansion in East–West trade. An action committee has drawn up its own plan to keep the works open. Some jobs would still be lost, but a vocational training centre would train displaced workers for new jobs and the bulk of the workforce — 3000 men — would still be kept on at the plant. Maxhütte would become a modern recycling plant turning scrap into specialist steel. The plan would not be cheap. It could cost anything between DM350 and DM5000 million. Sacking 3000 Maxhütte workers would cost DM207 million including redundancy payments.

The alternative for Maxhütte workers is bleak. Closure would push unemployment up to 30–40 per cent: when CSU politicians said some 5000 jobs would be created in the area, local SPD councillors were as sceptical as the workforce. When the plant was declared bankrupt in April 1987 the social payments guaranteed by Klöckner to the 1135 workers who took advantage of the early retirement offer in 1983 abruptly ceased. They were not in the mood to be so trusting again. Many demanded evidence that real jobs, by which they meant similar ones to those they would lose, were to be provided. Younger workers also feared that they would be expected to leave their home town to seek reemployment elsewhere.

Their scepticism was founded on experience. Because of its location, industries moving to Oberpfalz are entitled to special inducements. The local council will pay 25 per cent of start-up costs, for instance. But as the leader of the ruling SPD group Gerd Geisman pointed out, those incentives only demonstrate that the location is highly unattractive. 'We've tried and tried,' he says, 'but everyone wants to set up in Munich, not out in the sticks. People think we are half way to Czechoslovakia.' Between 1972 and 1987 only 14 firms came to Salzbach-Rosenberg, creating a total of no more than 410 jobs.

To the north and south of Oberpfalz are troop exercise areas. To the east is a 40 kilometre wide border zone, where incentives are even higher than Geisman can offer. Up to 40 per cent of a company's costs can be met from public funds. The region's image has been dented further by the construction of the highly controversial Wackersdorf nuclear processing plant. Demonstrations and violent clashes with riot police made television news headlines. The TV pictures provided stunning anti-nuclear propaganda, but bad publicity for the area. Among the jobs the CSU-dominated state government offered Maxhütte workers were positions as guards at Wackersdorf. They were furious.

Workers complained that when new industries move in, there are few jobs and most of them are not for men. Near the Maxhütte works is a small modern industrial estate. Only a handful of workers are employed there. Steel workers are not poor. At DM14.50 an hour, most have a fairly comfortable lifestyle which they cannot hope to maintain easily, even if they could find a job elsewhere. Ernst Makitta, 28, is a member of the shop stewards' committee and the SPD. He lives in a tastefully decorated rented flat with his wife and six year old son and drives a BMW. His brother is also a steel worker, and like many at the plant, a part time farmer. His wife works in a trouser factory. If Maxhütte is shut down for good, 'It will be the poorhouse for people here,' he says. Already people are leaving the towns. Many at the plant took advantage of a company offer to buy houses they rented from the firm. They have little chance of selling them now.

Ironically, there has been no shortage of interest in the plant. Other steel firms put forward a plan for joint purchase. But

149

workers were understandably sceptical about the plant's future under such ownership. The most they could hope for was to end up as a finishing mill for crude steel brought in from elsewhere.

The Bavarian state government told workers it would be prepared to take part in such a rescue plan. Bavaria could take a 49 per cent stake in a restructured plant employing 1000 workers. But the Federal government would have to provide the finance. The view of the union, IG Metall, is that the private sector cannot be relied upon to keep the plant open. Nationalization is the only guarantee.

The Bavarian government attempted to take cover behind the EEC, claiming that its rules on competition forbade a stake of more than 49 per cent in the company. This was nonsense, as Competition Commissioner Peter Sutherland informed local MPs. The rules do not distinguish between publicly and privately owned firms.

Under political pressure, the Maxhütte receiver has agreed to grant the plant a reprieve until the end of 1988 on condition that 420 redundancies are paid for by the Bavarian government. Unless there is a change in the overall outlook for the industry, Salzbach-Rosenberg faces a bleak future. But the workers are in a mood to fight and have had the clout to win some concessions from the government to keep Maxhütte open. They have not lost their faith in the plant. But early on, they feel, others had — from Flick and Klöckner to the state government. And that has made their fight so much harder.

Bagnoli

If proof is needed that moving into high technology does not guarantee the future of a steel industry, consider the story of Bagnoli's ultra-modern steel plant. Built to replace the antiquated mill which used to stand on this site near Naples, it is Italy's first continuous casting mill, making coils for the canning industry. What it has never made, since it opened its doors in 1985, is profits.

When the old plant — belching its smoke into what once was a bathing resort for the wealthy — hit financial trouble in the crisis of the 1970s, the government was convinced that the future of this otherwise deprived region could be secured by a clean, modern, high tech plant.

Planners believed that the new Bagnoli plant, by turning out two million tonnes of coil to can Italy's tomatoes, would form part of a continuous production line for Southern Italy's most important export — food. It would become to Italian tomatoes what producers of blue wrapping paper were to spaghetti.

It took five years to build and cost £500 million. The old plant was scrapped. The mill was almost entirely automated. On the shop floor there is not a soul in sight: Bagnoli workers sit behind video screens in air conditioned control rooms, a far cry from the unbearably hot foundry shops of old. Some 13 per cent of the cost of the plant was taken up in making it clean. Scrubbers and filters were fitted to render the smoke harmless and waste discharges minimal. The killer dust which was once the main hazard for steel workers has been eliminated. Fish returned to the sea. The plant itself, surrounded by lawns, shrubs and trees in the care of a team of 20 gardeners, is a shop window for steel in a town where it has never been a popular industry.

The price paid by the workers who backed the modernization programme was heavy. Five thousand men took early retirement. The new plant employed only 3,500, some of them soon on short time because of the company's poor performance. Automation also dealt a heavy blow to the many workshops and subcontractors which had depended on the plant.

Despite the investment and the sacrifices, Bagnoli was never given a chance to prove itself. At full stretch the plant could have turned out 2.4 million tonnes of steel a year. EEC quotas restricted output to 1.2 million. On that basis it could never make a profit. In its first year it lost £68 million. By 1987 annual losses looked set to climb to £70 million. Over a third of the workers were on short time: one month on, one month off under a special government scheme which allowed them to continue drawing unemployment pay in their months off.

The government did everything possible to switch production to Bagnoli to save the plant. In the hope of persuading the EEC to grant the plant the quota increase it needed, 2 million tonnes of coil went out of production at Cornigliano. They also tried unsuccessfully to persuade private steel companies to make the necessary production cuts. But Brussels was unmoved. It insisted that plants be treated individually. It would not accept that cuts elsewhere were an argument for maintaining surplus capacity at Bagnoli. The only way out was to buy the quota off another firm. Falck were offered £225 million to close down their coil plant and hand over the quota to Bagnoli. They refused. Finsider, the nationalized industry which owned Bagnoli, was denied EEC grants until it agreed to allow the second reheating furnace to be shut down.

Unions at Bagnoli blamed private steelmakers for their plight. Using old-fashioned electric furnaces, they recycle scrap into wire and construction steel for export, thereby escaping the quotas which were stifling Bagnoli. The mainly Communist unions wanted to see these less productive plants shut down instead. As Giancarlo Federico, general secretary of the Naples CGIL union branch, said: 'If Bagnoli were inefficient, even we would be in favour of closure.' But the unions were also in a delicate position. They pushed through the modernization plan even though it cost 5000 workers their jobs. They could not give up the plant without a struggle when so much had been sacrificed to bring it into existence.

The plant cannot count on the support of all Bagnoli's inhabitants, who still complained of dirt and smoke even after the new, supposedly non-polluting plant opened. Many feel that the seaside town would be better off moving wholeheartedly into the tourist business. With at least three quarters of school leavers condemned to almost certain joblessness in an area where organized crime is on the lookout for idle hands, that would not by any means be the whole answer. One of the fifty-year olds who took early retirement, like most never to work again, summed up for many townspeople: 'We are not in love with steel, but we are against unemployment.'

Federico attacked the government for not standing up to the private industrialists and Brussels, whom he readily blamed for Bagnoli's plight. But the government found itself in a weak position. Many had advised against the construction of the Bagnoli plant. Both the Commission and the other Eurofer members, including BSC, thought it was madness when there was so much overcapacity around.

The decision to double the plant's capacity by adding a second reheating furnace, not included in the original plan, particularly angered Brussels. Few outside Italy were surprised that the bullish market projections used to justify the plant were not borne out. It never became a major supplier to the Italian canning and car industry as its architects intended. Northern Italian industrialists preferred to buy their hot rolled coil from the French mill of Fos-Sur-Mer, just along the Mediterranean coast. At Bagnoli they claimed the French were avoiding customs duties by reclassifying their steel as seconds.

When the Commission announced in 1987 that there were four or five hot rolled plants which had to go, there was little doubt that Bagnoli was in the firing line. The plant had been doomed from the start.

Ravenscraig

The 'all stations' train that runs from Glasgow out to Motherwell in Lanarkshire is like a procession through the graveyard of Scottish manufacturing industry. As the train emerges from the endless blocks of rundown council estates, it passes the abandoned sites of what once was a thriving steel and engineering centre. Disused machinery stands there rusting. Ceilings caved in, grass growing in the cracks. These were once the workshops supplying the Clydeside shipyards, the Linwood car plant and the Leyland truck works at Bathgate.

Today all that is left of Scottish heavy industry is the loss-making Govan shipyard and Yarrow. Male unemployment in the whole of the Strathclyde region in the industrial belt of central Scotland is nearly 23 per cent, the highest in the United Kingdom.

Just past Motherwell, the huge works at Ravenscraig looms into view. Its chimneys are about the only ones still emitting smoke. Planted there in 1953 as a result of Harold Macmillan's political choice of a site for the strip mills which would supply the then booming car and white goods factories in the region, it now stands like a condemned men on death row. British Steel, it was universally believed, wanted to close the plant. But for the Conservative government it would mean political suicide in Scotland.

One by one the major employers have left the area — first in a trickle, then in a flood. Ravenscraig has now become the symbol of whether Scotland has any future as a manufacturing centre. The government stood by when the Invergordon aluminium smelter shut in 1984, and again when the Gartcosh finishing mill closed in April 1986. The campaign to keep Gartcosh open gave the government a foretaste of what would happen if it tried to move on Ravenscraig itself. Only 11 miles away, it was a major consumer of Ravenscraig strip. The campaign to save Gartcosh was all-party. Local chambers of commerce joined churchmen and trade unionists in the fight to keep it open. The campaign bit deep into traditional Scottish Tory loyalties. The chairman of the Scottish Conservative Candidates Association resigned. One former Tory MP, Ian Lawson, left to join the Scottish Nationalists.

In the 1987 general election, whilst the Conservatives did even better across much of England than in 1984, the Scottish Tories were almost wiped out. Their representation halved, from 21 to just ten seats. There were no longer enough Scottish Tory MPs to staff the Scottish Office, and Scottish peers with no governmental experience were drafted in to fill the vacancies. Defence Secretary George Younger held on by the skin of his teeth, winning his Ayr constituency by only 182 votes. The Scottish Secretary Malcolm Rifkind was said to have threatened to resign if the mill was closed.

Living under threat of closure had become a way of life for Ravenscraig workers. In 1982 chairman Ian Macgregor wanted to close the strip mill and ship bulk steel to the United States instead. In 1983 Brussels told BSC to close one of their strip mills. In 1985, Macgregor's successor Bob Haslam once again raised the possibility of closure. The closure of Gartcosh appeared to pave the way for a move on the Lanarkshire strip mill itself. Bob Scholey, who took over from Haslam, made little secret of his preference for concentrating strip production at Llanwern in South Wales, and withheld the new investment Ravenscraig workers believe their plant needs. Opposition to the closure of the plant is universal in Scotland. It comes from every section of the popu-

154

lation and cuts across party lines. In 1985 the government was forced to guarantee that the plant would stay open for three years. Scholey was told to shut up. It was perhaps the only time since the miners were defeated in 1985 that the Thatcher government had needed, for purely political reasons, to override a decision to close a plant.

Despite BSC's haste to close it down, Ravenscraig was far from being a lame duck plant. Modernization and productivity deals with the workforce — secured, it is true, under threat of closure — made it one of Europe's most efficient mills. In 1972 it took seven man hours to produce one ton of steel. In 1987, it took just two and a half man hours. Llanwern could not match the quality steel being produced in Scotland using the continuous casting process. With two of its three furnaces fully manned, Ravenscraig was producing two million tonnes of steel. At full stretch it would produce up to 3.2 million tonnes. But it had returned to profit. The lower pound against the Deutschmark had helped the strip mill division as a whole back to profitability.

Industrial relations at the mill were excellent. Why then was the plant under threat? Union representatives in Scotland believed that management was prejudiced against Scotland and in favour of Wales. Ravenscraig, they said was deliberately allocated shorter production runs. The rolling mills were in desperate need of modernization, but Scholey would not release the necessary funds. Yet he was prepared to authorize the purchase of new equipment at Llanwern and Port Talbot to bring the plant up to the level already being achieved at Ravenscraig. British Steel's headquarters are in London. The General Steels Division is based in Scunthorpe in north east England. The Strip Division's offices are in Wales. Ravenscraig workers felt there was no one to stand up for them where it counted.

Most of Ravenscraig's former customers had fallen by the wayside. The closure of Linwood was a blow almost as severe as the decline of shipbuilding, once the pride of the Clyde region and a source of employment for 50,000 people in 1967. Recently, the figure had fallen to 5000. North Sea oil had been a major consumer of steel for platforms and pipelines, but the oil boom collapsed in the early 1980s with the slump in the oil price. More than half of Ravencraig's semi-finished output went to Gartcosh for finishing. After the closure it was sent to Shotton in North Wales.

In addition to the symbolic value of Ravenscraig, its closure would be a heavy blow to the region's already battered employment prospects. First, there are 3,500 employed at the plant itself. In the mid-1970s the plant employed 8,500. Together with the 800 employed at Dalzell, where Ravenscraig steel is turned into heavy duty plate, 1400 at the tube factory at Clydesdale, and 100 at the Hunterston deep water port where the iron ore is landed, there are 5,500 jobs on the line in the Scottish steel industry. A further 35,000 jobs would go with them, particularly in the rail and road haulage firms, industries supplying the plant's power and even local authorities. But the blow to the region's morale would be more devastating still.

As 1987 progressed, the likelihood of an EEC closure programme receded. Instead, it looked as if controls were on the way out. Although as a matter of political form the Commission had to reject Britain's arguments that it was exempt from further closures because it had already made enough sacrifices, it was clear that the heat was on the Italians and the Germans. Commissioner Karl-Heinz Narjes, visibly irritated after successive lobbies by Ravenscraig workers had dragged him into what he saw as a domestic political quarrel, announced that the decision to close was in the hands of London, not Brussels.

Mr Kenneth Clarke, the minister responsible for British Steel, then announced that the company was to be privatized. The 1985 guarantee was replaced by a statement that BSC market projections predicted a demand for Ravenscraig steel for another seven years. The threat had receded — but who could be sure that market projections would not be revised? The unions were unsure whether the collapse of attempts to draw up a steel closure plan was good news. BSC argued that the strip division was being held back by quotas. If BSC seized a bigger market share, there would be more for Ravenscraig. But a collapse in prices would revive fears for the plant's future. Ravenscraig is a long way from London, still further from Brussels. No one knows that better than the Scots themselves.

Coal: The Cost of Closure

When the British National Union of Mineworkers was forced to call off its national strike after many bitter months in 1985, the defeat was felt not just in the communities in Britain for whom it had been a life and death struggle, but across the coalfields of Europe. If anything, away from the political divisions which embittered the strike for the miners themselves, support was more uncritical in the coalfields of Belgium and France than at home.

The defeat was seen as a setback for all European mining communities. Jan Olyslaekers, a leader of the Belgian miners who organized collections to support striking miners in the UK, had no difficulty justifying his stance. If the National Coal Board (later renamed British Coal) managed to push through its pit closure programme, there would be nothing to stop the same thing happening elsewhere in the EEC. Later events were to bear him out. In 1984 a chapter of Belgian working class history had closed when Roton, the last coal mine in Wallonia, shut for good. A long, bitter battle to preserve what was left of the Belgian collieries — the Kempense Steenkoolmijnene in Limburg — was to begin.

In Britain some of the mines flooded during the strike were never to reopen. Others were simply shut down and the workers transferred to other pits or into early retirement. The number of pits had fallen within three years from 170 to 100. Manpower had shrunk by 45 per cent. It looked as if by 1990 West Germany and Britain would be the only significant coal producers in the Community.

The decline of coal, like that of steel, was a direct consequence of an altered pattern of economic growth which had cost it substantial business. Steel, the biggest single user of coking coal, was contracting rapidly. Other industries had switched to cleaner, more transportable energy sources — electricity and gas. The oil crisis had put a halt to the trend towards greater use of imported oil and stressed the importance of coal as Europe's main indigenous energy resource. But by then there were other sources of energy, particularly for power generation. Both the EEC and its member governments — particularly France, Belgium and the

UK, and latterly West Germany — favoured the expansion of nuclear power generation during the Sixties and Seventies. By the time public disquiet about the safety of nuclear programmes had set in, reinforced by the disasters at Three Mile Island in the US and Chernobyl in the USSR, the plants had come on stream and the programmes were difficult to put into reverse.

But the problems of coal ran deeper than those of steel. Subsidies to steel makers were, in most EEC countries a relatively recent phenomenon. Coal has not been a paying proposition for many years. European coal is mined almost entirely at deep levels. It is a complicated and expensive process. Governments have for the most part recognized that and subsidized the industry in order to keep open mines which a pure profit and loss calculation would have closed. West Germany had a tax to encourage the use of domestic coal for generating electricity. Even the United States required power stations to use domestic coal. The alternative was to accept a larger degree of dependence on imported energy supplies than most countries thought desirable. The two oil price shocks of the 1970s seemed to confirm that this was a sound decision.

But it was a costly policy. When governments opted for austerity policies to curb public borrowing, support for coal came to seem an expensive luxury. The Coal and Steel Treaty made all subsidies illegal. This rule had been ignored. Governments continued subsidizing regardless.

As long ago as 1976, the Commission demanded an end to subsidies. Governments had agreed to phase them out in ten years. Nothing like it happened. In 1985 internal papers leaked to the West German press gave a taste of what Brussels was planning when the existing regime ran out.[5] To be fair, it was a preliminary report. But its plan to phase out the subsidies then being paid was deeply embarrassing to the Commission, which had to retract. It would have meant closing all British pits bar the main South Yorkshire/East Midlands coalfield, almost the entire Belgian industry, and the coalfields of Pas de Calais and Centre Midi in France. In Germany it would have meant closing down collieries in Aachen and Lower Saxony and part of the Ruhr coalfield. The report argued that half of coal production (about

100 million tonnes) in the Community was uneconomic. Rather than subsidizing the remainder, the Community would be better off buying cheaper, imported coal and switching the resources into the newer industries. Capacity would be cut by 15 per cent immediately to be followed by a phased closure programme covering 33 per cent of present capacity.

Because of the outcry, the report never saw the light of day. Instead, the existing policy was rolled over until 1993, with commitments to review it then. But with the main coal producing countries all pursuing pit closure programmes, it was hard to believe that the plan did not represent some kind of hidden plan for the industry. It certainly stated openly what many in power were thinking.

Nevertheless, the case for a subsidized European coal industry, was a great deal stronger than for other troubled industries. The coal companies themselves had gone along with closure plans, but generally believed that a decision to pull out of coal for good would be regretted in the long run.

European coal had a very specific problem. As British Coal's commercial director Michael Edwards told a commission of inquiry held by the European Parliament in the autumn of 1987, the main threat came not from failure to maintain its competitiveness, but from developments in the world market that were beyond its control.[6]

Oil companies like Exxon, sensing that coal would regain its price edge after the oil price shocks of the Seventies, had bought into coal very heavily. But they had overestimated the likely growth in demand. They invested in low cost open cast mining in countries like Colombia where there was no home market, hoping to break into the really big export markets in Western Europe and the Pacific. They miscalculated. Most coal is produced for domestic consumption and whilst the amount of coal traded internationally rose from 20 million tonnes in 1973 to 133 million in 1986, this was no more than 4 per cent of total production.

Production costs were low: open cast mining requires little specialist technology and labour in South America was cheap. But so was South African coal, thanks to the vast reservoir of cheap black labour, while coal from Eastern Europe was almost certainly being sold at a loss to earn desperately needed hard currency. Following the 1986 oil price fall, coal prices slumped to $30 a tonne in Western Europe. As recently as 1981, when strikes in Poland disrupted coal production, the price had scaled $80.

The Commission tended to assume a static market, but other forecasts showed that such an assumption could be damaging. There were grounds for suspecting that the multinational companies who owned the Colombian and other export mines would pull out in the face of continuing losses. Once the price recovered, uneconomic European mines would be viable again.

In any case, relying on imports was a very risky strategy. It would be playing into the hands of multinationals pursuing classic loss-leading tactics to gain a foothold in the European market. What is more, some economists reckoned that given the importance of the Western European market in international trade, a rise in its demand for imported coal would in itself be enough to force prices up. Europe would be very vulnerable.

Michael Edwards drew attention to a crucial distinction between coal and other industries. Coal mines cannot be shut down and started up again at will. Once a mine closed it would never reopen. In the 1960s, Europe had made the mistake of running down coal because oil was a cheaper, easily available energy source. When in 1973 the oil price rocketed and interest in coal revived, there was not enough productive capacity left to meet the surge in demand. The gap was met by increased imports. Europe was in danger of making the same mistake again.

That was not the only argument against phasing out subsidies. Two academics, George Kerevan and Richard Saville, demonstrated that far from releasing money for more production use, the 'close and import' plan which some governments were following, even without EEC agreement, would actually increase public spending by £2.6 billion.[7] Although their study was paid for by the Labour Group of Euro-MPs, British Coal itself used many of the arguments advanced in its own case against the British government. The case arose when government attempted to deprive British Coal of its one guaranteed customer for British steam coal, the Central Electricity Generating Board.

Sullivan and Kerevan advocated an alternative coal plan. It

160

involved perfectly justifiable action by the Community against dumping by non-European producers on EEC markets, an anti-pollution tax to encourage the use of low sulphur coal (widely available domestically) over high sulphur coal (mainly imported) and an EEC trading agency to even out short term fluctuations, especially those caused by wholesalers and stockholders.

But their challenge went a lot further. They included in their calculations the cost of maintaining half a million unemployed miners who would otherwise have been gainfully employed producing coal and paying taxes, but would have little prospect of finding new jobs in the current economic climate.

That in itself is a devastating comment on the European strategy for the traditional industries. The social costs of the strategy have never been calculated. Coal miners, steelworkers, shipyard workers are all being asked to pay that price. But the market economics which still dominates the thinking of most governments has not yet worked out how to take that price into account.

The powers granted to the EEC under the Treaty of Rome are less extensive than those granted by the Treaty of Paris which set up the coal and steel community. This has not prevented the development of a European policy for the shipbuilding and textile industries, but has shaped the way those politics evolved. The Community can intervene in these industries by using its power to regulate competition: it is authorized to control state subsidies. As in its approach to coal and steel, however, it has relied mainly on its own subsidization policy to enforce restructuring.

Shipbuilding The Tide that Didn't Turn

The pattern of decline in the shipbuilding industry mirrors that of steel. The recession of the 1970s hit the industry hard and in 1976 the Commission declared a crisis. As with steel, under the Fifth Directive subsidies by governments to keep uneconomic shipyards open were to be curtailed. But the contraction was to be orderly, not panic-driven. As long as closure programmes pushed ahead, subsidies could stay, provided they were not used to distort competition between EEC yards.

Faced with cheap ships from Korean and Japanese yards and a

slump in world trade which was reducing demand for ships, there seemed no choice. Only a leaner industry, where possible special-izing in technologically advanced ships, stood a chance of survival in that climate. The cure was painful — and it did not work. In ten years, shipbuilding capacity was slashed in half at a cost of 120,000 jobs.

By 1986, when the Commission drew up its plans for the Sixth Directive, the industry should have been emerging blinking into the bright sunlight of new orders and restored competitiveness. Instead, all that had happened was that Europe had a smaller industry.[8]

Far from following the EEC's example, Korea and Taiwan had bucked the slump by investing in new highly efficient capacity. For the cheaper bulk carriers and oil tankers, Far Eastern yards now had a competitive advantage of as much as 50 per cent. Meanwhile, forecasts of tonnage required have been revised steadily downwards. The demand for new tonnage in 1986 was estimated even by the Japanese as being no more than 12 million tonnes.[9] Brussels had projected 20 million tonnes when the Fifth Directive was drawn up. What had seemed ten years previously a mere demand trough had now become the pattern for the future. The new growth industries of the eighties did not produce large cargoes to be shipped around the globe. With a massive surplus tonnage pushing freight rates down through the floor, shipowners could not afford to buy new ships.

A cut of over a third would be needed to restore the industry to 70 per cent capacity utilization. That would mean 50,000 jobs lost by the end of the decade. Brussels reasoned that even in the areas where European yards could still compete, they would need a 26 per cent subsidy to be able to meet Far Eastern prices. That would have to be the cut-off point. Any yard which could not compete without a higher subsidy would simply go to the wall. After some jibbing, led by the Italians, the Directive went through at the first attempt. The subsidy war continued, however. Govan, on the Clyde, lost a ferry order in 1987 because a French subsidy broke the agreed ceiling. France was ordered to pay back the extra, but it was too late to cancel the order.

Euro-MPs, in a report written just before the Directive was

adopted, criticized the Commission paper as defeatist and negative in tone.[10] They thought the EEC could still persuade Far Eastern yards to cooperate by cutting back on capacity.

Specializing has not provided the answer to competition from that quarter, either. The collapse of the oil boom was a bitter blow to those yards in Scotland which had been converted to oil rig construction. In December 1986 Scott Lithgow, one of the most famous names in shipbuilding, announced it would have to close with the loss of 1500 jobs.

The theory that new technology could provide a competitive edge, despite the higher costs of European yards, has been a vain hope. For one thing, Japanese yards were already in that game. For another, the capabilities of the South Koreans and Taiwanese had been underestimated.

Textiles: Hanging by a Thread

Technology also kept alive the hopes of the EEC's textiles industry. Through the BRITE programme, the Community was pouring funds into the search for new technological processes that would make it profitable to manufacture in Europe again. That there was any industry at all was largely due to the Multi Fibre Arrangement (MFA) which, since 1974, has limited Third World exports of textiles and clothing to Europe.

It is the only traditional industry which benefits from overt protectionism, an option the EEC has rejected in its efforts to secure the future of more strategic industries. But few Third World countries, despite their long-standing dissatisfaction, were in a position to oppose the MFA — even when it came up for renewal in 1985. The arrangement had the support of the United States and other industrialized nations, even though it runs totally counter to the free trade spirit of the GATT agreement, from which they obtained a special exemption. European markets were not at risk from the technologically advanced Far Eastern countries (with the exception of Hong Kong). Cheaper textiles come mainly from very poor countries, like India, China and Egypt, who could ill afford to lose the markets denied them by the MFA.

Laser cutters and computer-controlled patterns and dyes offered the chance of a competitive industry that did not rest on a proliferation of backstreet sweat shops, exploiting immigrant labour to recreate in European cities the unacceptable conditions that prevail in the Third World. But once again people were being asked to make way for machines, as so often in this story. Where the jobs have gone is an easy question to answer. But where are the new jobs going to come from?

Nervously Into the Nineties

Job generation, in the Community as elsewhere, depends on economic growth. Towards the end of the 1980s, in spite of a modest period of economic recovery after the recession of the early 1980s, unemployment throughout the twelve EEC countries persisted at around seventeen million. Worse still was the prospect that a new world economic recession might push the numbers of people without work in the Community towards twenty million by the early 1990s.

The ascendancy of monetarist and free market economic policies during the 1980s was challenged only by brief and unsuccessful attempts at unilateral national economic expansionism in France and Greece. Indeed, we have seen that in 1987 there was even a move to dismantle the interventionist system of production quotas in the EEC steel regime. A majority of governments also appeared willing to place a greater degree of international trade liberalization on the agenda at the GATT negotiations in Uruguay. This would threaten sectors of manufacturing industry which have been under intense competitive pressure from outside imports.

Meanwhile EEC governments maintained an ultra-cautious approach in their overall economic strategy. Although they reduced interest rates after the stock market crash of October 1987, mainly in an effort to stem the headlong slide in the international value of the US dollar, their fiscal and monetary policy remained on the restrictive side of neutral. At the start of 1988, economic growth had slowed sharply in the Federal German Republic and several other EEC countries. However in Britain, where recovery had started from a more depressed level of activity, the government was able to report an unexpectedly strong rate of economic growth of around six per cent a year in 1987.

As far as the future was concerned most EEC governments were reluctant to take any initiative which might risk another inflation epidemic on the scale that swept the western economies in the 1970s – especially after the OPEC oil price increases. But international economic experts were already warning that a far greater danger was recession, and even outright economic depression, should the US Administration find itself unable to finance its budget deficit without significantly increasing interest rates.[11]

These arguments have been heard by the EEC Commission. Jacques Delors left the Copenhagen summit meeting of EEC heads of government in December 1987 in no doubt that failure to tackle the US deficit and the slump in the dollar could produce a major disaster.

The majority of EEC governments, however, remained uncertain about whether they should risk any radical change in policy when the outlook for the world economy remained so uncertain. The most significant development was increased pressure on West Germany to offset the impact of the Federal Republic's massive trade surpluses by reflating its economy, even if this involved some risk of inflation.

The overall economic philosophy of the European Community has four main elements: internal economic liberalization through the completion of the internal market; the strengthening of the European Monetary System; encouragement of cooperation in research and development, especially in the area of new technology; and a cautious fiscal and public expenditure stance.

The EMS has undoubtedly been one of the success stories of the European Community in the past decade. The most important measure of its effectiveness since it was launched in March 1979 has been the relative stability achieved in the relationships of those currencies taking full part in the system. Although exchange rate adjustments have occurred at intervals — invariably as a result of pressures on the EMS from outside, above all from the gyrations of the US dollar — they have been fewer and less disruptive than would have been the case had the EMS and the 'fixed exchange rate mechanism' (ERM) not existed.

A second positive development has been the increasing use of the European Currency Unit (ecu). Although its origins predate the establishment of the EMS, the ecu is not yet 'money' in the normal sense of coins or notes which can be tendered in a shop. It is, rather, a sophisticated European Community unit of account used in official government and other public sector transactions by the European Community, and in settlements between the EEC and a variety of bodies.

The ecu is made up of a 'basket' of EEC currencies. The different currencies are given a specific weighting within the ecu (which is reviewed every five years) and they have preordained values in relation to each other. The exchange rates of the ecu in terms of each national currency are published regularly and adjusted after each EMS currency realignment.

Under EMS rules currencies participating in the exchange rate mechanism (all the EEC currencies except those of Britain, Greece, Portugal and Spain) are allowed to fluctuate in value on world currency markets against the ecu. But this margin of fluctuation is relatively narrow — being 2.25 per cent of a central rate except in the case of the Italian lira which has a fluctuation rate of six per cent. When currencies threaten to breach these limits their central banks are obliged to intervene and defend them.

There are arrangements within the EMS whereby central banks can give one another assistance and — under strict conditions — intervene in support of another EMS currency should it come under speculative selling pressure on the foreign exchanges. Under the Danish EEC Presidency in the second half of 1987, this system of mutual support was enlarged, although it still falls far short of anything resembling a single European Community central bank responsible for the EMS.

One important criticism of the way the EMS operates is that the system is biased in favour of West Germany which has been by far the strongest economy in the EEC. The West German mark has thus tended to become the linch-pin currency around which the EMS operates. In practice this means that the EMS has had a somewhat 'deflationary' economic bias in that the major burden of currency adjustments has been borne by countries with weaker economies and currencies, who are required to deflate.

In the view of the majority of EEC governments, a more balanced and progressive system would place the onus of exchange rate adjustment at least as much on the mark. The West German authorities would then be obliged to pursue more expansionary policies, minimizing the danger of an overvalued mark pulling the rest of the EEC in an unduly deflationary direction. This argument, however, has always been rejected by the monetary conservatives who run the West German central bank. They attribute that country's economic success to the fact that counter-inflation has been an overriding policy priority.

This 'pro-German' bias has been cited by successive British governments as one major reason for keeping sterling outside the EMS fixed exchange rate regime.[12] But British reluctance also has much to do with entrenched hostility in Whitehall and the City to any arrangement which cedes sovereignty over economic policy to the EEC. Since the 1960s, exchange rate and interest rate policies have been among the most important weapons in the UK government's limited economic armoury, so this attitude is hardly surprising.

Nevertheless, pressure has been mounting on the UK to abandon its hesitations and join the full EMS exchange rate regime, particularly since the latest and most serious collapse in the value of the US dollar which began during 1986. In the view of the other EEC countries, the EMS will not be credible as an alternative pole for European currency and monetary policy until sterling is part of the system.

This view came to be accepted by both the British Treasury and the Foreign Office during 1987, but by the end of the year Prime Minister Margaret Thatcher was still holding out against joining. Supporters of the EMS believe that convergence between the economic policy objectives of the British and West German governments means that a decision to peg sterling against the other EMS currencies would have a less disruptive effect on British domestic policy than opponents of the fixed exchange rate regime have assumed.[13]

The worsening international monetary crisis of the later 1980s led the EEC Commission and others to press for more radical steps which would push the European Community further down the road to monetary union. But while there was a consensus in favour of strengthening the EMS and, possibly, of eventually creating a European monetary authority, resistance to anything smacking of supra-national EEC control of monetary — let alone fiscal — policy appeared as strong as ever.

It may be that political changes in EEC countries over the next few years will lead to more favourable attitudes towards monetary and even economic union. If the political pendulum swings away from ultra-liberal free market policies — perhaps under the impact of intensifying world monetary instability and a serious global recession — a consensus may emerge in favour of all-European monetary and demand management strategies.

Indeed, Keynesian economists, disillusioned by the experience of nationally based expansion strategies, have been turning their attention to collective, or at least coordinated macro-economic measures to boost output and employment. And increasingly the EMS has been regarded as a potential instrument to this end, even by economists on the left who in the past had regarded it as little more than a bastion of banking conservatism.[14]

Unless the EMS does evolve towards being a supra-national monetary authority, there will be a limit to the use of the ecu, the popular in private banking and commercial transactions in recent years.The ecu's real breakthrough will only come when it is a bona fide part of the national fiduciary issue in member states; that is, when it becomes a currency like any other.

The other striking element in the European Community's response to the economic and industrial crisis during the 1980s has been the emphasis on collaboration in technological research and development. This was born out of a growing concern about the dangerous technological gap that was opening up between industry in Western Europe and its more advanced American and Japanese competitors.[15]

The first step came after the publication of a French government paper, 'Technological Renaissance in Europe', in 1985. EUREKA was launched as a programme of civil research aimed at identifying, supporting and coordinating non-military industrial projects to secure the competitiveness of European high tech industries. Participation was not confined to the EEC, with countries such as Sweden playing an influential role. Although its non-military objectives were stressed, the immediate stimulus for EUREKA came when the United States announced its Strategic Defence Initiative. As we have seen, SDI or Star Wars provided another massive boost to the already formidable advantage enjoyed by US firms in the high technology field. It is interesting that EUREKA research programmes have no discernible social objective and are held by some critics to involve a potential and sometimes an actual military spin-off.

Eureka has a private enterprise base with very limited government or public sector funding. Its projects are strictly commercial in orientation and cover five programmes: large computers, third generation robots, wide band communications, ceramic turbines and high speed trains, and biotechnology applications. In addition it concerns itself with high technology applications in factories and in the home, and with the formulation of common European standards to underlay a single market in public procurement.

The EEC Common Science Policy was launched as long ago as 1974, establishing the principle of Community involvement in the research and development programmes of the member states. It was reappraised in 1980 and the first five-year programme was drawn up in 1983.

In 1987 a second five-year programme with a budget of £3.6 billion was agreed after important sections had been bitterly opposed by the British government. The new programme embraces ESPRIT (information technologies), BRITE (collaboration in pre-competitive industrial research) and RACE (telecommunications technology research). Other programmes deal with research into technologies for transport, biotechnology, industrial materials, health and other specialized applications.

These programmes and EUREKA do not exhaust European scientific and research cooperation. There is also the JET (Joint European Torus) programme which is researching energy from nuclear fusion — mainly at Culham, near Oxford. Other research bodies include the European Science Foundation, located in Strasbourg, the European Laboratory for Particle Physics (CERN) located at Geneva, the European Molecular Biology Laboratory at Heidelberg, the European Southern Astronomical Observatory at Munich and the increasingly important European Space Agency which has 14 European member states and an annual budget of more than $1.2 billion.

The size and overall impact of the EEC's R&D programmes should not be exaggerated. National governments resist substantial increases in the annual EEC budget allocation for research and development. Indeed, UK opposition to the five-year research programme proposed in 1987 caused a major row. Substantial reductions were made to certain sections before the programme was adopted.

More radical critics point to the domination of the EEC programmes by big European multinational companies. They argue that a far higher proportion of a bigger EEC research budget should be devoted to research based on Community needs rather than short-term profit-driven priorities. Some have pointed out that in Japan more attention is given to the research requirements of social sectors such as the environment, health, education and housing.

The ESPRIT programme does make space for research programmes which offer alternative views of the place of technology in industry and society. It is nevertheless true that the bulk of European research is driven by the imperatives, whether separate or combined, of profit and armed security. This is an imbalance bound to lead to continuing debate in the years ahead.

If the commitment of the European Community's member states to common research and development remains a modest one, this is even truer of EEC involvement in areas of economic activity such as transport, energy and the environment. Although some useful policy directives have been prepared and adopted in all these fields, the Community as such plays a marginal role by comparison with the national member states.

This is a reflection of both the modest size of the European Community budget — in all it accounts for less than one per cent of the member states' gross production — and the derisory sums allocated for non-agricultural purposes within the budget.

Although some objectives can be achieved without financial resources — such as common standards for environmental protection and international cross-frontier commercial traffic — these areas will not make any appreciable contribution to the wider goals of reviving the European economy and putting the peoples of Europe back to work without collective investment in the Community's infrastructure.

For most of its history the European Community has been administered on the assumption that trade liberalization and the mere removal of barriers to human, social and economic intercourse would be sufficient to ensure full employment and internationally competitive industry. Strategies based on conscious intervention in the economy, whether at a Community or national level, have been out of favour. This laissez faire approach has inspired the internal market liberalization to which EEC governments have committed themselves in recent years.

Some of its results have been impressive. As we have seen a significant amount of industrial restructuring has taken place — and both individuals and communities have paid the price. Old industries have all but disappeared and some new ones have emerged. In the place of coal, steel, shipbuilding and textiles, new industries and services — some based on the new information technologies — show only faltering signs of developing.

Whatever the pros and cons of industrial restructuring, unemployment remains the unacceptable face of contemporary Western Europe. The failure of the liberalization strategy to restore anything approaching full employment will surely be high on the European political agenda at the start of the 1990s. A new debate on European growth strategy is beginning. On the left, voices are being heard advocating new, more flexible and international forms of public sector economic intervention. There are already proposals to give public sector agencies at local, regional, national and European levels a greater role both in stimulating demand and in tackling the investment constraints on the economies of the European Community.

7
European Futures

We have seen that external pressures demanding greater European integration are likely to outweigh internal conflicts of interest as the European Community enters the 1990s. In that sense the collapse of the EEC and the 're-Balkanization' of Europe seem very remote prospects. Nevertheless, the immediate future is by no means assured. The internal budget conflict goes to the heart of the kind of Community which the member states want to see over the next decade or so. It is not impossible that the budget crisis could get out of control, and then some of the internal policies which have bound the twelve together might start to unravel.

The full impact of the budgetary crisis has yet to be felt in the agricultural industry. But already in the latter months of 1987 there were signs of growing political discontent among farmers facing loss of revenue and even bankruptcy. The setbacks suffered by the centre-right coalition government in Denmark in the general election of 1987, as well as the losses of the right-wing Christian Democrats in Federal German state elections like that in Schleswig Holstein during the same period, were attributed by observers to a backlash of disillusioned and discontented farmers.[1]

The farming vote has even more significance in southern Europe, and it remains to be seen whether governments in these countries will be able to stay the course of CAP reform, if the agricultural vote swings against them. There will be great pressure on national governments for state subsidies to make good the loss of open-ended EEC price support. More subsidies would do little, however, to deflect farmers' anger, while destroying the common agricultural market which the CAP evolved.

The target of completing the EEC internal market by the end of 1992 may also turn out to be too ambitious. While all national governments are ready to give general support to the goal of a barrier-free EEC market, it may prove another matter when they come to approve detailed deregulation proposals which hit hard at the interests of specific social or economic groups.

Already the suggestion that the twelve correct the existing disparity of VAT levels, creating two broad bands of tax, has aroused great controversy. Opposition is fierce both from countries — such as Britain — which traditionally have been hostile to the notion of taxing certain commodities such as food, and from governments who have long depended on the revenue from high VAT rates, such as Greece.

It would be surprising if the poorer, southern European countries agreed to abandon all controls over the free movement of capital. Neither will governments — in the rich as in the poorer EEC member states — readily abandon national industrial subsidies, as West German reluctance to end state aid to its coal-mining and other troubled industries has shown.

Nor will all national governments freely abandon control over the movement of individuals and their right to work in the profession of their choosing in the Community. One problem already looming is the existing agreement of the Nordic Union countries, under which citizens of Denmark, Finland, Iceland, Norway and Sweden can travel freely in each other's countries.

Under the internal market proposals Denmark will be obliged to extend the right of free movement to all other countries of the EEC. This could mean that Finns, for example, would be able to travel without hindrance of passport formalities from Helsinki to Lisbon, or that a Greek could settle with equal freedom in Iceland. Compromise solutions will probably be found to these and other problems, but the completion of the internal market may be slowed in the process.

Some of these internal difficulties could be eased by the future expansion of the membership of the European Community, though the obvious candidates — Turkey, Cyprus and Malta — bring with them a range of economic, political and social problems.[2] But there are also indications that most — if not all — of

173

the six richer member states of the European Free Trade Association are reconsidering their positions on entry into the Community. In the closing months of 1987 there was speculation that Norway might begin tentative negotiations about membership after its next general election, due in 1989. Recent opinion polls in Norway suggest a reduction in the numbers of people opposed to EEC membership, by comparison with the referendum of 1972. And in the intervening years some of the problem areas — notably fishing policy — which were influential in the outcome of the vote in 1972 have been resolved on terms favourable to Norway.

An active debate on EEC membership has also begun in a number of other EFTA states. Following the publication of a government White Paper on the subject in Norway, a similar exercise was undertaken in Sweden. Although it concluded that serious obstacles remained — notably Sweden's traditional foreign policy neutrality — it also underlined the growing extent of common economic interests between Sweden and the EEC.

In Sweden, Austria and Switzerland, a strong feeling has developed among industrialists that the completion of the EEC internal market could pose serious problems for countries remaining outside — not only as regards obstacles to trade, but also through the imposition of new technological and industrial standards which the internal market process will determine.

It is too soon to predict whether the neutral status of Austria and Switzerland (and the unique constitutional position of the Swiss Confederation) will prove insuperable obstacles to EEC membership. It certainly does seem unlikely that Finland — given its special relationship to the Soviet Union — would enter a NATO-dominated Community.

On the other hand Soviet attitudes to the European Community are changing. It now seems only a matter of time before the European Community is formally recognized by COMECON, the eastern bloc's economic and trading organization. This would be a major development, in that only a few years ago, the official line of the Soviet Union and its Warsaw Pact allies was that the European Community was a creation of the United States. The eastern bloc states resolutely refused to recognize it or its institutions, insisting that all diplomatic and commercial relations were with the individual national governments of the EEC countries.

The first break in this attitude came when Romania signed a commercial cooperation agreement with the EEC in 1978 similar to that negotiated earlier by non-aligned Yugoslavia. Then in 1987 negotiations were opened with Hungary for an equally ambitious cooperation agreement, and the EEC prepared for talks about more cautious trade links with most of the other Eastern European states as well as the Soviet Union itself.

The Soviet Union and its allies may no longer have any particular interest in holding back the Western European 'neutrals' from membership of the EEC when they themselves are keen to forge closer links. The authorities in Moscow seem to have concluded some time ago that the European Community is by no means a tool of American Cold War foreign policy, but rather an economic and political grouping with its own interests which sometimes clash sharply with those of the United States.

These developments may make it easier for the EFTA countries, or some of them, to join the European Community between now and the end of the century. Their comparative prosperity would bring significant relief to the Community's hard pressed finances, and that could prove crucial in developing policies to aid the poorer EEC countries in the years ahead. Even if the EFTA states do not immediately sue for entry into the EEC, they have left no one in any doubt that they want closer cooperation with the twelve — above all, over the development of the internal market. But if the EFTA states stand to gain a great deal by being consulted over the abolition of trade, capital and fiscal barriers in the EEC, what would the Community expect to get in return?

The EEC twelve are far more important to the EFTA six, than the other way round. The Community already benefits from EFTA participation in common technological and industrial research programmes, such as Eureka (already organized on an 'all-Western European basis') or specifically EEC programmes such as ESPRIT or BRITE. It would be surprising if the EEC countries did not press the EFTA states to make an indirect contribution to the economic development of the poorer, mainly southern European, member states. While full membership would be a more clear-cut solution to the dilemma of EFTA–EEC relations, this might provide a second-best compromise.

Either way it seems that the eventual emergence of an EEC–EFTA industrial bloc, with a market of some 350 million people, is likely. Might it also be that a European Community of eighteen full or 'associate' member states would be in a far stronger position to implement protectionist 'Fortress Europe' economic policies, if the 1990s do prove to be years of even deeper international recession? Such a large economic bloc certainly would be less vulnerable to international economic sanctions from other advanced economies.

It would be wrong, however, to underestimate the overtly *political* appeal of the Community to the remaining non-members in Western Europe and, to a degree, those in Eastern Europe as well. The development of EEC political cooperation — and with it the prospect of a common foreign and security policy — is itself a magnet, though of course there are contradictions in this process. At any moment in time, a European foreign policy depends on who makes up the individual governments in the EEC member states. At the moment a right-wing consensus exists on foreign and defence policy issues, but this might well change between now and the year 2000. Whatever standpoint the European Community adopts on East-West relations, nuclear disarmament, policy towards South Africa or Central America, or any other issue, there is a general desire throughout Western Europe (and maybe parts of Eastern Europe) to have a greater collective influence in world affairs. In Western Europe this desire is spurred by growing dissatisfaction (for sometimes contradictory reasons, as we have seen) with the United States and its leadership of the Western Alliance.

Unease about the future direction of US policy on defence and disarmament has revived interest in what is known euphemistically as 'a stronger European pillar of NATO' but which in reality is an attempt by Western European states to define their own security strategy. Reluctant to undermine the foundations of NATO, they have wanted to channel the revived debate on European defence through the Western European Union rather than through the European Community, which includes one neutral — Ireland —

and two suspected by their allies of being 'semi-neutral' — Denmark and Greece. The WEU also has the advantage of being a forum which does not include the United States.

The revival of the WEU in the early 1980s aroused Washington's unease. As we have seen, America's European allies have been warned of the dangers of undermining NATO unity. But since the Reykjavik summit in 1986, when many NATO governments felt their views on nuclear arms reductions were being ignored by the US, and the signing of a super-power agreement eliminating European land based medium range nuclear missiles, there has been a renewed stress on the need for a specifically 'European' security strategy.

It is beyond doubt that should an INF agreement between the United States and the Soviet Union be ratified, and should speculation about a rundown in the scale and character of America's commitment to the defence of Europe continue, European political and security cooperation will become increasingly significant. The more obviously military aspects of European security cooperation might, initially at least, be restricted to the seven nations in the WEU. But in the longer run, and especially if the European Community progressively absorbs the remaining Western European countries, security policy would come to depend almost inevitably on EEC political cooperation.

Already the distinction between WEU and EEC political cooperation is crumbling, as was evident during the period of Belgian presidency of the EEC in the first half of 1987. By virtue of holding the presidency, the Belgians discussed with the United States both foreign policy and security issues which strictly were the province of the WEU. This tendency alarms the US even more than the revival of the WEU as such. For the present, at least in public, the line on both sides of the Atlantic is that the integrity and stability of NATO is beyond doubt. But, as we have seen, this optimism is not shared throughout the higher echelons of the NATO alliance.

The price, therefore, of a more positive and coherent European foreign and security policy may be a progressive weakening and even the eventual replacement of the Atlantic Alliance. This, of course, will not happen overnight and it is bound to be affected by the political line pursued by the next US President and by any changes in the political character of the European governments during the 1990s.

Should the right continue to hold sway in Western Europe, then it is possible that a new security relationship will be established with the United States. This could be based on a new division of labour in the field of defence, possibly including some 'European' controlled nuclear arms capacity. If this released US military resources to be deployed in other areas of the world, such as the Middle East — as the former US Security adviser, Mr. Zbigniew Brzezinski, has suggested — then the new relationship, though changed, might remain relatively amicable.

On the other hand it is possible that the decline of US military involvement in Europe, combined with the important if limited super-power agreement to eliminate medium range nuclear missiles in Europe, will encourage demands for European disengagement from the structures of the Cold War. In most West European countries, but perhaps most strikingly in West Germany itself, there is support for the politics of non-alignment and for positive political steps to overcome the division of Europe.

Any trend towards neutrality in Western Europe during the 1990s would certainly hasten a break with the United States and have repercussions on NATO. Whether or not this might be matched by parallel changes in Eastern Europe it is too soon to say, but even now there are signs of a growing demand in Eastern European countries for greater independence from the Soviet Union (even under the more liberal Gorbachev regime). The inevitable effect of commercial agreements with the EEC, as Romania and Yugoslavia learned from the agreements they negotiated in the early 1980s, is that their economies will become even more 'open' to the capitalist world system.

The East European governments hope that this openness will aid their economies through direct investment, increased loans from the West and the acquisition of west European technological know-how. There is no doubt about their need for such aid. At the end of 1987 the outlook for the economies of Poland, Czechoslovakia, Hungary, Romania and Yugoslavia was bleak in the extreme. There were plans for extensive price increases in most of these countries as part of an industrial restructuring programme which, it was predicted, would also result in significantly higher unemployment and lower living standards.

As we have seen there is considerable interest in Western Europe, and in the Federal Republic in particular, in the exploitation of the huge potential market for European consumer goods in Central Europe. But the West German foreign minister, Mr Hans-Dietrich Genscher, warned on several occasions during the late 1980s that increased intra-European trade might require an aid programme for Eastern Europe on the same scale as Marshall Aid for western Europe in the late 1940s.

The political environment for such a radical evolution in intra-European relations will obviously be influenced both by the general state of the western economies (which could make the eastern bloc economies look even more attractive in the 1990s) and by the general climate for relations across the Iron Curtain. But this will depend on whether Mr Gorbachev and his reform strategy survive intact in Moscow and are strong enough to overcome internal opposition — not just within the Soviet Union, but also within the ruling bureaucratic regimes in Russia's East European client states who are markedly less keen on political democratisation than they are on economic liberalisation.

The other key factor will be the extent to which the governments of Western Europe, through the EEC and NATO, are ready to move beyond Cold War thinking and use the possibility of drastic reductions in military forces in Europe to negotiate a new political settlement in central Europe including the withdrawal of both NATO and Warsaw Pact forces. At the start of 1988, the attitude of the key West European states, notably Britain and France, was cautious in the extreme, although even the centre-right coalition in Bonn seemed ready — in the words of Franz-Josef Strauss, after a visit to Moscow in December 1987 — to recognise that 'we have moved beyond the Cold War era'.

Which road Europe takes will not be decided solely by the debate about foreign and security policy. It is bound to be influenced by the climate of transatlantic economic relations. If the 1990s are years of economic recovery and a progressive return to full employment, of international trade liberalization and monetary stability, it is less likely that the economic fault lines in the present relationship between Europe and America (or indeed Europe and Japan) will turn into a full scale rupture.

Conversely, should the 1990s prove to be years of continued 'stagflation' — episodic periods of recovery interspersed with new recessions — and years of continuing high unemployment, trade imbalances and protectionism, the transatlantic relationship could go into crisis. Gloomy auguries on global economic prospects for the 1990s were far more common than optimistic ones.

The nature of the world economy over the next decade will also have a crucial influence on the internal economic policy followed by the European Community. At the end of the 1980s liberal free market economic policies continue to hold sway, but are unlikely to survive if unemployment resumes its upward trend in the early 1990s. In spite of the commitment to complete the EEC internal market and to abolish all remaining barriers to free trade and capital movement by the end of 1992, a reaction taking the form of economic *dirigisme* and protectionism in one or more EEC countries cannot be ruled out.

It is even possible that the political pendulum will swing sufficiently far to the left in enough EEC countries to persuade the European Community as a whole to adopt a different strategy during the next decade. New forms of supra-national public sector intervention and cross-frontier economic planning could become fashionable.

Sections of the European left and labour movements have begun to discuss a democratic, planned economy for Europe between now and the year 2000. They are considering new agencies for public sector intervention in the affairs of multi-national companies, together with a new emphasis on local and regional public sector initiatives — some modelled on experiments by left-wing regional and local authorities during the early 1980s. The stress on quantitative targets for economic growth and employment in the centre-left strategies of 1960s and 1970s is now seen as inadequate unless greater attention is given to the nature of growth itself and the social priorities it implies. The Green and feminist movements are influential in shaping these alternative economic strategies: so too are those radical trade unionists who

demand 'socially useful' production, 'human centred' manufacturing technologies and democratic participation in the planning
of enterprises at the local, national and European levels.

Conferences of European trade unionists have been held in
recent years to discuss campaigns for the 35 hour week, as well
as the wider issue of flexible time working, a subject of specific
interest to women. There is also growing trade union interest,
most notably in Denmark and West Germany, in technologies
that maximize the input and contribution of human skill; and
pioneering work on the first human-centred, computerised manufacturing system has been led by the technology division of the
Greater London Enterprise Board, a development agency set up
by the now defunct Greater London Council.

Production geared to social needs has been much debated in
European labour movement circles in recent years. It has grown
out of the initiative of British Lucas Aerospace trade unionists,
who responded to the loss of jobs in arms production by developing an alternative plan, using their skills and knowledge to
produce goods needed by a wide range of disadvantaged groups.

Serious attention is now being paid to the concept of socially
useful production by economists sceptical of a profit-driven market
economy's ability to restore full employment. This approach to
economic regeneration rests firmly on a widening of democracy in
economic and industrial life. There is a growing body of workers'
experience, in countries as diverse as Britain, France, Sweden and
Switzerland, of attempts at forms of democratic control of the
enterprise. And the GLC sponsored a more comprehensive
approach to popular local and regional planning, which has since
been studied closely in other EEC countries.[3]

In discussing the possible futures which Europeans may
confront in the 1990s, little attention has been paid so far to
national perceptions of the EEC. Any review of the future of
Europe which ignores these national realities risks being hope-
lessly abstract. Yet in recent years economic integration and
exposure to the same basic problems have brought about a
remarkable convergence in popular attitudes to European issues.

Today, there is less starry-eyed idealism about the Community
in those countries — Belgium, Holland, Italy and West

181

Germany — where there was most popular support for European federalism in the post-war decades. To judge by the evidence of reports on popular attitudes published by the European Commission, cynicism and boredom are as much to blame as any revival of old-fashioned nationalism in these countries, although the situation in West Germany is ambiguous.

Growing numbers of Europeans, especially in these 'heartland' states, find the Community less relevant to their problems and aspirations, and casually convict it of bureaucratic ineptitude and political failure. A large minority see it as weakened by years of internal strife and stagnation.

In the Benelux states and Italy, popular 'European' aspirations remain stronger for a mixture of historical, cultural and economic reasons. The Belgian and Italian centre-right governments were reluctant to adopt the Single European Act because they felt it did not go far enough down the road towards eventual economic and political union.

Neither is 'Europe' an issue dividing left and right in these countries. Some of the more zealous advocates of a revived European federalism have been found, in recent years, in the ranks of the Italian Communist Party, rather than on the right. In none of these countries, even on the far left, is there any echo of the demand still heard in Britain for national withdrawal from the Community.

One reason for this is the relative lack of legitimacy of the national state in both Belgium (because of deep seated linguistic and regional rivalries between Dutch speaking Fleming and French-speaking Walloons) and Italy (partly because of the long period of Fascism between the wars). But there is also no doubt that Belgium, Holland and Luxembourg have been exceptionally well placed to exploit the potential for increased trade and multi-national investment, since they formed the original heartland of the European Community.

In West Germany the souring of the EEC ideal seems to have gone furthest. In addition to the reason given above, this is a reflection of the growth to maturity of two generations of West Germans who have no memory of Nazism and feel no personal guilt for the atrocities of the 1930s and 1940s. In the past, some

Germans substituted 'Europeanism' for a German national identity they rejected.

Both the right and sections of the left have shown a renewed interest in German reunification in recent years. More people feel that the Federal Republic has the right to assert its 'national interests' with the same degree of energy as the other EEC countries, both within and outside the Community. Over the past thirty years the Federal Republic has rarely questioned the fact that, as the richest and most powerful industrial member state of the EEC and the one with the greatest vested interest in the development of a European Market, it should pay the lion's share of the costs of the Community. Now, however, West German public opinion has become much more sceptical about whether Bonn is getting 'value for money' in the EEC.

Ironically, more criticism of the wastefulness of the Common Agricultural Policy has been aired in the Federal Republic than in any other member state except the UK. But many of the worst features of the CAP, as we have seen, were the result of determined lobbying by the powerful farm lobby within successive West German coalition governments. The Federal Republic is unlikely to be an effective promoter of reform until these internal differences have been settled.

Indirectly, disillusion with the EEC also reflects the tarnishing of the German 'economic miracle' in recent years. Not only has economic growth slowed in the Federal Republic but many of its traditional mass employment industries — such as coal and steel — have been hit hard by restructuring.[4]

For all these reasons a section of German public opinion wants to reduce the financial burdens arising from the EEC budget. Others urge the pursuit of international policies with less regard for the susceptibilities of Community partners. West Germany, they believe, should be less inhibited in forging a new economic, and possibly a new political relationship with the Soviet Union and the countries of '*Mitteleuropa*'.

The emergence of Mikhail Gorbachev and the Soviet Union's strategy of '*Perestroika*' and economic reform, including encouragement for joint economic ventures between west European industry and the Soviet state, has excited considerable interest in the Federal Republic. It remains to be seen whether the Soviet system can restructure itself sufficiently to justify joint ventures on a scale that would require a major reorientation of West German policy.

For the moment the West German political establishment insists that, whatever opportunities for a new relationship with the eastern bloc are opening up, there is no question of downplaying let alone abandoning their commitment to the European Community and to the Atlantic Alliance. Given the enormous importance of the European market for German industry, there is no reason to question the Federal Republic's continuing commitment to the EEC.

The future relationship of West Germany to the Atlantic Alliance may prove more problematic. The right-of-centre coalition of Christian Democrats and Liberals is far from united on future policy towards nuclear arms reductions and how far this should be determined by NATO and US priorities. The opposition Social Democrats now reject the 'First Strike' doctrine and support a major break with NATO nuclear orthodoxy, while the Green Party, with the support of a significant if minority section of public opinion, wants a complete break with NATO's integrated military command.

There are unresolved ambiguities in West German attitudes to the European Community. But while Left and Right have very different ideas about the future of the European Community, there is little dissent from the view that West Germany's future, and an end to European and German divisions, should be pursued in close association with the countries of the EEC. It is worth noting that the Federal Republic may well insist on a less narrow focus on the Community as it seeks new commercial and political openings in eastern and central Europe.[5]

In some ways the history of France's association with the EEC is the reverse of the West German experience. From the beginning French public opinion was uncertain about the political role of the European Community. These reservations first surfaced when France refused to enter the European Defence Community in the early 1950s. They found full expression during the ascendancy of de Gaulle a decade later.

It was not that de Gaulle and his supporters doubted the economic case for a Common Market and European integration, rather that they refused to contemplate any development which would diminish the sovereignty of the French state. This attitude was shared by a section of socialist opinion and even by the powerful French Communist Party of the 1950s and 1960s.

The crisis over majority voting within the EEC Council of Ministers and the decision to leave NATO's integrated military command in the 1960s drew the line that defenders of national sovereignty in the French establishment refused to cross. It was part of a nationalist world outlook embracing an unqualified commitment to nuclear energy and nuclear weapons.

The European Community which has evolved over the past twenty years is indeed closer to de Gaulle's '*L'Europe des Patries*' than the embryo of a federal United Europe envisaged by the Community's founders. It could be argued that this prevented political frictions between national member states and the European institutions, which might have proved fatal to the Community in its tender years.

On the other hand it imposed the pace of the 'slowest camel in the train' on economic (let alone political) integration. This, in turn, has slowed EEC responses to rapidly changing economic and political circumstances.

Over the past ten years the Gaullist position on the EEC has been in decline in France. Today even the neo-Gaullist party is far readier to contemplate supra-national solutions to problems facing the Community, while the French conservatives, the Socialist Party and the radical left (though not the increasingly marginalized Communist Party) support European integration in their different ways. It is no coincidence that the member state with the most serious commitment to the completion of the internal market has been France.

This process is, however, uneven. The French are uncertain whether, for example, they really wish 'Europeanization' to supersede outright national sovereignty in defence policy. However the right-wing government of Jacques Chirac has come closer to a rapprochement with NATO, and at least a symbolic reintegration of French and West German armed forces, than would have seemed possible a few years ago. The French, more than most, recognize the limitations of the post-war Atlantic settlement and that Europe's interests are bound to diverge more and more from those of the United States. But they are reluctant to pursue an alliance with the West Germans alone as the foundation for a new European security policy.

That is why parallel efforts are being made to interest the British in closer cooperation on nuclear defence. In the view of some French strategists this might eventually include the development of a joint nuclear force to replace American missiles withdrawn from Europe under agreements with the Soviet Union. However in reaction to this development a French anti-nuclear lobby — grouped around the ecologists and the far left — is seeking common ground with the semi-neutralists and peace movements in other parts of Europe.

As far as the EEC itself is concerned, the prospect of an unrestricted common market has stimulated some French socialists to argue the case for policies to parallel if not to offset the effects of Community-wide economic liberalization. Such a programme would include major transfers of resources to the poorer regions and a concerted strategy for economic growth and full employment, with measures to counter financial speculation and tax evasion.

The trends are less clear-cut in the three newer member states. For the great majority of Greeks, Portuguese and Spaniards through the 1960s and 1970s, joining the EEC was part and parcel of the struggle to overthrow dictatorship and establish the roots of parliamentary democracy. For that reason, the EEC has not been as divisive an issue as it might have been, given the abrasive effect of the Common Market on the still fragile economies of these countries. The waning of this early enthusiasm surrounding entry, and the culturally liberating association with a wider Europe which it brought, has resulted in rising discontent with the EEC.

Much will now depend on the precise impact of the internal market and the effectiveness of the measures taken to produce greater economic cohesion between richer and poorer countries of the Community. However, in Greece and Spain attitudes have been embittered by the austerity measures introduced by both governments. It is not clear whether the EEC is blamed for such policies.

The enlargement of the Community to twelve member states has increased the political clout of the poorer, mainly southern European Community states, though this is only effective when they stand and vote together in the Council of Ministers. In the capitals of the northern European states it is commonplace to hear predictions that, over the next few years, the European Community will inevitably undergo a process of 'creeping Mediterraneanization'. By this is meant a tilting of the political agenda within the Community towards the issues of social and regional development.

The arithmetic of voting rights within the Council of Ministers does not, however, reflect the true strength — or rather, weakness — of the newer member states. Their position would be stronger if, individually or collectively, they could point to a credible alternative to EEC membership. They also lack the bureaucratic experience and skill necessary to manipulate the levers of power in Brussels to their advantage. The older and richer member states, by contrast, have always taken good care to ensure that their interests are represented by well-trained and talented officials. The southerners could prove, however, to be a 'spoiling minority', slowing down the momentum of liberalization and integration. Thus far there has been little debate within the southern bloc on an alternative path of development for the EEC.

Of the other three member states, Ireland remains the most 'Europeanist', in part because EEC membership has provided a welcome alternative focus to the unhappy relationship with Britain. As the Irish President, Mr Patrick Hillery, told the European Parliament in October 1987, 'in more recent centuries [the long period of British occupation] events conspired to impede the cultivation of the natural affinities between Ireland and the continent of Europe'.

The years immediately after Irish entry into the EEC in 1973 brought remarkable economic growth, and access to the Common Agricultural Policy resulted in a tangible boost to depressed Irish farm incomes. As a member of the Irish government reportedly

187

said during this period, 'each night I kneel down and say a prayer of thanks for the CAP'.

Until recently support for the EEC has been overwhelming in the Irish Republic, with opposition limited to a small group on the religious right, militant republicans and sections of the far left. By the early 1980s, however, something of a reaction had set in: the deteriorating state of the economy, with its chronic indebtedness and failing manufacturing base, was having a devastating impact on Irish industry, employment and living standards. The curbs on EEC agricultural spending were also beginning to bite into the incomes of poorer farmers. Disillusion is also fed by the relative failure of the Community's regional and social development policies to raise Irish living standards nearer the EEC average.

Some of these frustrations manifested themselves in 1987 when the Single European Act was put up for endorsement in a referendum made necessary by an Irish Supreme Court ruling that the SEA might limit the government's unfettered right to determine its own foreign policy. Though the SEA did not change the basic character of European political cooperation, there were signs that some Irish politicians were anxious to reconsider Ireland's traditional neutralism and this acted as an alarm bell for nationalists, republicans and socialists. They were worried at what they saw as a drift away from the state's traditional policy of non-alignment in the Cold War and towards implicit support for the NATO alliance. The referendum was carried by a majority after an ill-tempered public debate. While it was clear that the voters were solidly behind continued EEC membership, the size of the opposition also reflected disillusion with the country's economic and social situation.

Ironically, in a referendum on the same issue held a little earlier the Danes had endorsed the Act by a larger majority than any gained in previous votes on EEC issues. Danish reluctance over EEC membership — second only to the United Kingdom's, up to now — has stemmed partly from traditional links with the rest of the Nordic world. But it has also reflected a certain defensiveness about Denmark's generally higher standards of living, social provision and care for the environment, and the opposition of a sizeable proportion of the population to any move which might make the EEC an extension of the NATO bloc. In the years since 1973, however, a growing number of Danes have concluded that the EEC is not necessarily a threat to these values and loyalties. In Denmark, as in other countries, it has become more and more difficult to conceive of purely national, let alone isolationist, solutions to the economic ills besetting the country.

Danish influence within the EEC is out of proportion to its size or the strength of its economy: in particular, the Danes are recognized as the champions of environmental and other standards in the EEC. The 1987 general election saw a swing towards support for radical foreign and security policies, including a degree of dealignment from NATO. If this trend is confirmed in the next election — which might follow quickly because of the inconclusive outcome of the 1987 vote — a left government may well be elected. Conceivably, such a victory could begin a trend elsewhere in the EEC, especially if by then there is dissatisfaction with the priorities of the completed internal market.

It is more difficult to judge the mood in Britain. The evidence suggests that much of the bitterness has gone out of traditional political opposition to the EEC, though this may be merely a measure of people's boredom with the whole subject. Certainly the partisans of a European future for Britain are still few in number, uncertain as to their base, and inhibited about expressing their views.

There is less European zeal in the party which took Britain into the EEC in 1973 than there was two decades ago. In the Conservative party the traditionally pro-European 'wets' have ceded place and influence to the supporters of Thatcherism who regard positive participation in a European future with icy reserve. Of course the party and the government accept EEC membership as an inescapable fact of life, and an opportunity for those financial and other services better adapted to a wider European market than manufacturing industry. But there is little in the way of warmth towards the wider potential of a supra-national Community.

This graceless acceptance of EEC membership has found its most potent expression in the style adopted by Mrs Thatcher herself in her often bruising exchanges with other Community leaders. Some may argue that this is an unintended, unfortunate side effect of the argument over Britain's financial contributions to the EEC budget which has persisted throughout the Thatcher years. But it goes deeper than that.

Margaret Thatcher and her admirers in the Tory party are without doubt European 'minimalists'. They see some virtue in a Common Market, much less in a Community, and none at all in the idea of a Union. In a sense Thatcherite Conservatism has inherited the mantle of Gaullism and the notion of a Europe strictly '*des Patries*'.

This is not the only factor which makes British Conservative attitudes towards the Community somewhat jaundiced and sceptical. The British, and by no means just the Conservatives, remain 'mid-Atlanticists'. Of all the EEC countries, the United Kingdom is the least willing to contemplate any radically new relationship between Europe and the United States, let alone a rupture in the Atlantic Alliance itself.

British politicians believe, or at any rate purport to believe, in the continued existence of the much vaunted 'special relationship' between London and Washington. There is — in the age of the new US economic nationalism, of SDI and the new isolationism — no real place for such a relationship. It is a piece of theatre with which the US indulges successive British governments, but which has no real purchase on the modern world.

Strangely enough this Atlanticism is shared by the Labour party leadership, which explains the otherwise eccentric attempt by Neil Kinnock to sell his party's unilateralist nuclear defence policies to a hostile Reagan Administration on the eve of the 1987 general election. The resulting, all too public disavowal of Labour by Washington embarrassed and confused a party which still seems to believe in the primacy of its commitment to NATO.

While the Conservative party has moved in a neo-Gaullist direction, the Labour Party has progressively abandoned any serious commitment to withdrawing Britain from the Common Market. The reasons are not difficult to find. None of the alternatives which Labour offered in the past as a substitute for EEC membership — association with EFTA, links with the Commonwealth, the special relationship with the US — has stood the test of time. After the 1983 election defeat less and less has been heard of withdrawal and its corollary: the isolationist strategy of a national siege economy. In its place, and especially after the 1987 defeat, has come gradual, grudging acceptance of EEC membership. So far as the leadership and a strong body of party opinion is concerned, EEC questions are of secondary importance. This shows up in the lack of effective party guidance for Labour members of the European Parliament and in its lacklustre relations with sister parties in the Confederation of European Socialist parties.[5]

A slight warming of official Labour Party attitudes was signalled in a letter sent by Neil Kinnock to the chairperson of the European election committee of the Confederation in December 1987. In the letter Kinnock for the first time stressed the importance of agreeing a common election manifesto to be shared by all the EEC socialist parties and made no reference to existing Labour Party commitments to negotiate withdrawal from the Community.

There is no doubting the serious threat which the proposed completion of the internal market poses for any future national government with a mandate to intervene in the free market system to achieve desired economic or social ends. If such a government is elected in the 1990s, in Britain or elsewhere, conflict with the EEC Commission and the Rome Treaty appears inevitable. The outcome of any battle over intervention would depend on the pressure which the European allies of such a government could mount in its support.

The Labour left is also uncertain about its future strategy. Clearly it regards the Treaty of Rome and the completion of the internal market as a threat to traditional Labour policies on economic planning, public ownership, regional and other subsidies, and equal opportunities policies. The unanswered question is, how does it propose to counter this threat?

There are, however, signs of reviving interest in positive European strategies to defend jobs, economic expansion, a higher general level of social services and welfare, and other working-class interests.[6] The opportunity clearly exists for the beleaguered left to open a new political front, encouraging an alternative attitude to Europe agenda to the qualified Gaullism of the

Conservatives or the rather bland, traditional pro-Common Market stance of the Liberals and Social Democrats.

Of course, if the British left does try to seize this opportunity, it will have to break down traditional suspicion of supra-nationalism within its own ranks. It is not possible, for example, to press for pension benefits closer to those of Denmark, or unemployment benefits closer to those of West Germany, without accepting the need for a far broader distribution of income and wealth within the European Community.

Who is to effect that redistribution if not a more powerful, reconstructed European Community? At present the British left is unsympathetic even to the call for a more powerful European Parliament, rejecting the present Community institutions and the Treaty of Rome as reflections of the interests and values of capital. But what alternative does it propose, faced with the clear inadequacy of the national state as a vehicle through which to effect fundamental economic and social change?

Indeed, this is the dilemma for all the different British political parties. Developments in the world economy and in the Atlantic Alliance's security strategies in recent years make it difficult to see how the European Community can hold its ground unless it wields the authority of a semi-state. The European Monetary System, for example, will not be able to ensure greater monetary stability in a highly unstable global monetary environment without greater power to intervene in the markets and to enforce a far closer coordination of the various national economies. Sooner or later, the European Community, whether through the EMS or some other body, will have to be given a stronger role by the centre-right governments to ensure the progressive convergence of the management, fiscal and public spending policies of the various national entities.

Up to now, nothing more than a difference of emphasis has separated those who advocate a full 'Common Market' and those who talk the language of a 'European Community'. This period may now be drawing to a close. In the 1990s, it may well be that this distinction will constitute a fundamental choice between different ways of life, different notions of 'freedom'. And increasingly this choice will be faced by voters who are willing or reluctant

'Europeans'. The strict free marketeers do not *need* new institutions or new treaties; those who advocate the building of a European Community — let alone full economic and political union — will be obliged to go out and win support for an entirely fresh look at European strategy.

The elements of such a strategy are already visible in demands for greater rights for workers and consumers and for an ecologically and socially–costed growth strategy. The voice of the consumer's organizations, coordinated through the BEUC organization in Brussels, has already been influential in legislation on toy safety, and on pollution.

There is also a growing movement of opposition to industrial farming and in favour of environmentally conscious organic farming. The crisis of overproduction in agriculture and the fact that the old system is now totally discredited means that the arguments of what, in the 1970s, was still a fringe of activists are now being listened to by many more people.

We have looked at the work done in recent years on a new approach to technology, socially-useful production and on new forms of popular planning. Although traditional forms of state ownership are discredited in the eyes of both left and right, there is interest in new forms of public ownership, not only at a local, regional and national level but also — for instance in the proposal for a European Community Enterprise Board — at the international level.

Studies are being carried out into new social policy strategies which would build on the highest level of benefits and entitlement obtaining in any one country. This, of course, implies a gradual evolution towards a Community taxation policy, and assumes the development of a Community monetary and central banking function, whether or not this can be achieved through the existing European Monetary System.

Indeed, it is possible to hope that the citizens of a more democratic and humane Community would witness a liquidation of the Cold War military alliances. The reunification of the torn halves of Europe might then become more than a dream.

Notes

Notes to Chapter One

1. The former United States Supreme Military Commander of NATO, General Bernard Rogers, has said he does not expect (US forces in Europe) 'to remain in the present strength for ever'. He added there was a danger that withdrawal might take place 'overnight'. (*The Guardian*, November 6, 1986). The newly-appointed US Secretary of State for Defence, Mr Frank Carlucci, told Reuters that he could not guarantee that pressure on US military spending, because of the need to reduce the Federal Government's budget deficit, might not lead to US troop withdrawal from Western Europe (*The Guardian*, November 1, 1987).
2. These aspirations were strikingly demonstrated during the official visit by the East German leader, Mr Eric Honneker to the Federal Republic in October 1987.
3. An opinion poll carried out by Eurobarometer for the EEC Commission in November 1987 showed that in Britain and Denmark suspicion and resentment of EEC plans to abolish national barriers to free trade and freedom of movement were significantly higher than in the other ten member states.
4. See my 'Cost of Withdrawal From the European Community', Royal Institute of International Affairs, London 1982.
5. The SEA provided for a number of decision making procedure. While widening the application of majority voting, some key matters — for instance, taxation — must still be handled on the basis of unanimity.
6. This was very much the tenor of discussions at the ministerial level meeting of EFTA member states held in Interlaken, Switzerland, in June 1987.
7. Cited by Michael Newman in *Socialism and European Unity*, London 1983.
8. In the aftermath of the British general election of 1987, leaders of the Labour Party, who had hitherto supported eventual withdrawal by the UK, stressed the fact that Britain would remain in the EEC for a considerable time, and emphasised the need to work for change with other parties of the left in Europe.
9. Eden's address to Columbia University, January 11, 1952.
10. *Financial Times*, June 15, 1962.
11. Indeed the Copenhagen European Council of December 1987 met for two days but failed to agree on a budget for 1988 and any longer term reform of

the Community's finances. As a result the EEC entered 1988 on an emergency budget with a real prospect of money running out later in the year.

12. The European Community welcomed the tentative agreement between the Reagan Administration and the US Congress in December 1987 on reductions in the \$30.2 billion budget deficit projected for 1988 and \$45.9 billion for 1989. But there were doubts about whether these cuts would be enough to reduce significantly America's calls on the western world's savings to finance its expenditure.

13. The telecommunications industry's internal liberalization plans have not yet been matched by a willingness to negotiate common technical standards with Japan and the US. In the absence of such standards, American and Japanese companies will find it difficult to exploit fully a more open European market.

14. Some of these issues are dealt with in the report *European Business Strategy to 1990*, European Research Associates, Brussels 1986.

15. For example a meeting of the WEU Council of Ministers in The Hague in October 1987 effectively discouraged Spain from formally applying for membership — because of its refusal to accept a nuclear element in NATO's military strategy.

16. Such a poll was reported in the *Sunday Telegraph*, December 6, 1987.

Notes to Chapter Two

1. The welcome decision of December 7, 1987, to liberalise European airtravel, will alas have very little impact on the increasingly used routes between Brussels and the other EEC capitals.

2. For an interesting account of these early days by one of the 'Founding Fathers' see Jean Monnet, *Memoirs*, London 1978.

3. De Gaulle, *Memoirs of Hope*, London 1971. For Hallstein's view on these and other controversies of the first decade of the Community see *The European Community*, Dusseldorf (Econ Verlag) 1979.

4. In the aftermath of the failure of the European Council of EEC heads of government in Copenhagen in December 1987, both the Commission and the European Parliament threatened to take the Council to the European Court.

5. A recent insider's account of life in the Commission is that of a former British commissioner, Christopher Tugendhat, *Making Sense of Europe*, London 1986.

6. A useful account of the complex institutional geography of the European Community is contained in John Paxton, *Dictionary of the European Communities*, London 1984.

7. See 'Making a Success of the Single Act: A New Frontier for Europe', Spokesman's Service of the European Commission, Brussels, December 1987.

8. See Anne Robinson, 'The Public Image of the European Parliament', Policy Studies Institute, London 1986.

9. Robinson, op. cit.

10. An interesting account of the influence of the European Court of Justice can be found in *The Wall Street Journal*, European Edition, October 3, 1987.

11. See John Robinson, ' Business Strategy to 1990', European Research Associates, Brussels 1986.

Notes

Notes to Chapter Three

1. For an examination of the wider economic debate and policy choices facing European governments see Stuart Holland, *Out of Crisis*, Nottingham 1985.
2. Robin Murray, 'Ownership, Control and the Market', *New Left Review* 164, 1987.
3. I have touched on some of these issues in my book *Europe without America* (Oxford University Press, 1987).
4. An excellent summary of some of these conflicts is contained in Andre Gunder Frank, *The European Challenge*, Nottingham 1983.
5. See W. Hanrieder, in William Diebold Jnr (ed.) (Winthrop Publishing, Cambridge, Mass., 1974).
6. This charge was specifically levelled by the EEC in response to American criticism of European government subsidies for the European Airbus project during 1987.
7. See Hanrieder, 'The United States and Western Europe'.
8. The Americans charged a number of West European and Japanese firms with violating the COCOM ban on the export of sensitive equipment to the Soviet Union. Some of these charges were admitted. In response, in November 1987 the US Administration proposed a marked tightening of these legal controls in return for liberalization of trade in such items between the COCOM member countries.
9. Independent Television, Channel 4, December 1986.
10. *The Guardian*, March 3 1987.
11. Cited in the Military Committee report to the North Atlantic Assembly, 'NATO — Warsaw Pact Military Balance', September 1987.
12. Thus Lord Carrington, NATO Secretary-General, among others (*The Independent*, December 1, 1987).
13. See December 1987 issue of *END Journal*, organ of the European Nuclear Disarmament movement.
14. Prominent among Administration spokesmen taking this line was Assistant Secretary for Defence Richard Perle.
15. Independent Television, Channel 4, 'Inquiry into the State of NATO', September 29, 1986.
16. *The Independent*, January 16, 1987.
17. 'France and U.K. move closer to joint missile', *The Guardian*, December 15, 1987.
18. Cited in an article in *The Spectator*, July 1985.
19. Reference to an 'Evil Empire' was first made by President Reagan in a speech to the National Association of Evangelists on March 8, 1983.
20. Certainly traditional Reagan Administration 'hawks' such as Perle (see note 14) were strong supporters of the INF Treaty.
21. Cited in John Connell, *The New Maginot Line*, London 1986.
22. Set out in NATO's 'Airland Battle' and 'Follow on Force Attack' strategies.
23. Independent Television, Channel 4, 'Inquiry into the State of NATO'.
24. *The Guardian*, November 6, 1986.
25. See Socialist Society/Campaign Group of Labour MPs, 'The Case for Withdrawal from NATO', London, March 1986.
26. See the Garluzzi report on European Security, presented to the European Parliament, October 1987.

27. Mrs Thatcher speaking to the House of Commons, December 9, 1987.
28. Assessment published by the International Institute for Strategic Studies, London, November 1986. The WEU assessment was published by the Committee on Defence Questions and Armaments, and was prepared for the Western European Union Parliamentary Assembly, Paris, November 1987.
29. This was made apparent in testimony given to a public hearing on 'New Ingredients in European Security Policy' organized by the Political Affairs Committee of the European Parliament between November 30 and December 1, 1987.

Notes to Chapter Four

1. Report on behalf of the Budgetary Committee of the European Parliament (A/254–87) May 1987.
2. *Wall Street Journal*, October 15, 1987.
3. Data provided by the European Commission, Brussels.
4. This aspect of the CAP is dealt with interestingly in a special report on 'Options for European Agriculture', published by AGENOR in Brussels in May 1986.
5. John Paxton, *A Dictionary of the European Communities*, London, 1982.
6. This aspect of the CAP is amusingly covered in Richard Cottrell, *The Sacred Cow*, London, 1987.
7. *Financial Times*, London, November 24, 1987.
8. Commission answer to Ms Christine Crawley, Labour Member of the European Parliament, November 24, 1987.
9. A comprehensive account of the different CAP support mechanisms is included in 'National Policies and Agricultural Trade', OECD, Paris, 1987.
10. *Financial Times*, London, October 17, 1987.
11. Alan Matthews, 'The Common Agricultural Policy and the Less Developed Countries', Trocaire, Dublin, 1985.
12. Warnings to this effect were delivered to the European Commission during 1987 by a number of senior Reagan Administration officials, including, in December, the US Secretary of State, Mr George Schultz.
13. Among the growing number of public bodies trying this approach, the London Food Commission has been prominent.

Notes to Chapter Five

1. 'Eurobarometer', European public opinion surveys, June 1987.
2. 'Completing the Internal Market', White Paper from the European Commission to the European Council, June 1985 (Com (85) 310 final).
3. 'The Post Magazine' and 'Insurance Monitor,' reprinted in *Kangaroo News* 15, April 1986.
4. Reported in *Kangaroo News* 22, October 1987.
5. id. reprinted from *Newsweek*.
6. Parliamentary Question No 108/85 by MEPs Seibel, Emmerling, Sabellarion, Rothley, Vittinghof.
7. *Kangaroo News* 15, April 1986.
8. *BEUC News* 68, October 1987.

Notes

Notes to Chapter Six

1. See Max Bellof *The United States and the Unity of Europe*, London, 1963.
2. This is explicitly spelled out in Article 2 of the Principles of the Treaty of Rome.
3. General Objectives Steel 1990 Com (85) 208, Commission Working Document.
4. Steel Policies, Commission Communication to the Council Com (87) 388.
5. Coal Policy Commission Papers Com (85) 251, 525.
6. European Parliament Committee on Energy, Research and Technology: 'Towards a European Policy for Coal', submission by M. I. Edwards, Commercial Director, British Coal.
7. 'The Case for Retaining a European Coal Industry' by George Kerevan and Richard Saville with Debra Perceval.
8. Orientation paper on future aid strategy for shipbuilding, Communication from the Commission to the Council Com (86) 324.
9. Proposal for a 6th Council Directive on Aid to Shipbuilding. Com (86) 531.
10. European Parliament Committee on Economic and Monetary Affairs and Individual Policy Draft Report on 6th Directive on aid to shipbuilding (Com (86) 531) — PE 109.291.
11. See the statement of forty distinguished international economists — *The Herald Tribune*, 15 December 1987.
12. See article by Professor Sir Alan Walters, economic adviser to Mrs Thatcher, *The Times*, 24 April 1986.
13. See *Financial Times*, 9 September 1987, p. 25.
14. This was the theme of contributions made by leading British and other EEC socialist economists at a conference on 'Alternatives to Trade Wars', London, November 1987.
15. See 'The current State of Western High Technology', paper presented by Giles Merritt to a conference, on 'High Technology, Western Security, and Economic Growth' held in Brussels, February 1986.

Notes to Chapter Seven

1. The Belgian general election in December 1987 provided evidence that the political swing to the right had gone a little into reverse. The primary beneficiaries of losses sustained by the Christian Democrats were the French-speaking wing of the Socialists and the Dutch-speaking wing of the 'Greens', although the right-wing Flemish liberals also made some gains.
2. The decision of the Turkish government to apply for EEC membership in 1987, was given a frosty response by the twelve. It seems that progress on the application will depend on substantial economic changes and a more unambiguous adoption of democratic political standards by Turkey.
3. See Hilary Wainwright, ed. *A Taste of Power*, London 1987; Robin Murray, ed., *The London Industrial Strategy*, GLC, London 1986; Mike Cooley, *Architect or Bee*, London 1987.
4. This development was dramatically underlined by the angry mass demonstrations of steel workers in the Ruhr during December 1987. Their plants were threatened with closure and the loss of some 20,000 jobs.

Notes

5. See *The Guardian*, December 28, 1987.
6. David Martin, *Bringing Common Sense to the Common Market*, Fabian Tract 525, London 1988. Martin is leader of the British Labour Group of MEPs. See also *Interlink*, journal of the Socialist Society, December 1987.

Glossary

BEUC

Bureau Européen des Unions de Consommateurs: European Bureau of Consumers' Unions.

COMECON

Council for Mutual Economic Assistance: eastern bloc development and trading organization.

Commission of the European Communities, commonly referred to as the European Commission

The policy-making executive of the EEC responsible for its day-to-day management. The commissioners, although appointed by member governments, are supposed to act independently of both governments and the Council of Ministers.

Common Agricultural Policy (CAP)

As set out in the Treaty of Rome, the EEC must operate a common market in agriculture. To achieve this the CAP regulates markets, prices, imports and exports. See Chapter Four for a full discussion.

COREPER

Comité des Representants Permanents de la CEE; Committee of Permanent Representatives of the EEC, or 'ambassadors' of the member states.

Council of Europe

A group of twenty-one Western European states concerned with cultural, legal and inter-parliamentary co-operation. The Council overseas the European Convention on Human Rights and the work of the European Court of Human Rights in defending basic liberties and rights.

Council of Ministers

The EEC body that brings together representatives of the national governments. It decides on the Commission's proposals. See Chapter Two.

European Development Fund

The EEC's fund for aiding the less developed countries.

ECSC

European Coal and Steel Community, founded in 1952 to develop a common market in these basic industries.

ecu

European Currency Unit. The ecu's value is determined by adding together a 'basket' of European currencies in certain fixed proportions. It is the basis of the EMS.

ESC

Economic and Social Committee. An advisory, tripartite body reporting to the Commission. Membership consists of employers' organizations, trade unions and other groups such as consumers and farmers.

EDC

European Defence Community. An abortive military alliance of the early 1950s. See Chapter Three.

EFTA

European Free Trade Association. The trading organization of non-EEC Western European nations: Austria, Iceland, Norway, Portugal, Sweden and Switzerland. Finland has associate membership.

EMS

European Monetary System. Set up in 1978 to provide greater monetary

201

stability among members of the community. Britain and Greece do not take part in the EMS. All other EEC countries must maintain their currencies' fluctuation within agreed limits.

ETUC

European Trade Union Confederation, association of national trade-union bodies from fifteen countries. Makes representations to EEC institutions on matters of interest to workers.

European Council

The meetings of EEC heads of government, which take place three times a year, are distinct from the Council of Ministers and are designed to discuss matters of general importance and great delicacy – such as budgetary reform.

European Court of Justice

Reviews and safeguards the application of Community Law.

European Investment Bank (EIB)

Independent organization charged with investment in less advanced regions of the EEC to ensure 'balanced development'.

European Parliament

See Chapter Two. A directly elected, consultative assembly of the Community.

GATT

General Agreement on Tariffs and Trade. An agreement, originating in 1948, that sets out guidelines for world trade and is regularly updated. Tries to overcome obstacles to the free movement of goods and services. Its 'rounds' are multi-lateral negotiations for the conduct of world trade. The latest is the 'Uruguay Round'.

JET

Joint European Torus. A torus is a

hugely expensive machine for experiments with thermo-nuclear fusion, so costly that it is financed by the Community as a whole. Situated at Culham in Oxfordshire.

MFA

Multi-Fibre Arrangement. An agreement regulating international trade in textiles.

OECD

Organization for Economic Co-operation and Development, bringing together the major countries of the developed world to co-ordinate economic and social policies.

UNICE

Union of Industries of the European Community. A European federation of employers' organizations.

WEU

Western European Union. A forum, dating from 1948, of European NATO members. See Chapter Three.